INSTITUTE OF LEADERSHIP & MANAGEMENT

SUPERSERIES

4 HOUR LOAN

FOURTH EDITION

Published for the
Institute of Leadership & Management by

Pergamon *Flexible* **Learning**

OXFORD AMSTERDAM BOSTON LONDON NEW YORK PARIS
SAN DIEGO SAN FRANCISCO SINGAPORE SYDNEY TOKYO

Pergamon Flexible Learning
An imprint of Elsevier Science
Linacre House, Jordan Hill, Oxford OX2 8DP
200 Wheeler Road, Burlington, MA 01803

First published 1986
Second edition 1991
Third edition 1997
Fourth edition 2003

Copyright © 1986, 1991, 1997, 2003, ILM
All rights reserved.

No part of this publication may be reproduced in any material form (including photocopying or storing in any medium by electronic means and whether or not transiently or incidentally to some other use of this publication) without the written permission of the copyright holder except in accordance with the provisions of the Copyright, Designs and Patents Act 1988 or under the terms of a licence issued by the Copyright Licensing Agency Ltd, 90 Tottenham Court Road, London, England W1T 4LP. Applications for the copyright holder's written permission to reproduce any part of this publication should be addressed to the publisher

British Library Cataloguing in Publication Data
A catalogue record for this book is available from the British Library

ISBN 0 7506 5816 9

For information on Pergamon Flexible Learning
visit our website at www.bh.com/pergamonfl

Institute of Leadership & Management
registered office
1 Giltspur Street
London
EC1A 9DD
Telephone 020 7294 3053
www.i-l-m.com
ILM is a subsidiary of the City & Guilds Group

The views expressed in this work are those of the authors and do not necessarily reflect those of the Institute of Leadership & Management or of the publisher

Authors: Howard Senter and Eileen Cadman
Editor: Eileen Cadman
Editorial management: Genesys, www.genesys-consultants.com
Based on previous material by: Howard Senter and Diana Thomas
Composition by Genesis Typesetting, Rochester, Kent
Printed and bound in Great Britain by MPG Books, Bodmin

Contents

Workbook introduction — v

1. ILM Super Series study links — v
2. Links to ILM Qualifications — v
3. Links to S/NVQs in Management — vi
4. Workbook objectives — vi
5. Activity planner — vii

Session A Delegation – a vital skill — 1

1. Introduction — 1
2. What does delegation mean? — 2
3. Why is it important to delegate? — 3
4. Objections to delegating — 10
5. Authority and responsibility — 11
6. The process of delegation — 14
7. How effective delegation will help you — 16
8. Summary — 20

Session B Achieving balance in delegation — 21

1. Introduction — 21
2. Under-delegation — 21
3. Over-delegation — 27
4. Identifying under-delegation and over-delegation — 29
5. Levels of control in delegation — 31
6. Summary — 35

Session C Preparing to delegate — 37

1. Introduction — 37
2. What should not be delegated? — 38
3. What should be delegated? — 39
4. Delegating to volunteers — 45
5. Which of your tasks can you delegate? — 45
6. Selecting a team member for delegation — 53
7. Summary — 60

Contents

Session D Carrying out delegation — 61

1. Introduction — 61
2. Setting objectives — 62
3. Planning — 66
4. Monitoring the delegated task — 72
5. Reviewing the delegation — 74
6. Summary — 81

Performance checks — 83

1. Quick quiz — 83
2. Workbook assessment — 85
3. Work-based assignment — 87

Reflect and review — 89

1. Reflect and review — 89
2. Action plan — 91
3. Extensions — 93
4. Answers to self-assessment questions — 95
5. Answers to the quick quiz — 98
6. Certificate — 99

Workbook introduction

1 ILM Super Series study links

This workbook addresses the issues of *Delegating Effectively*. Should you wish to extend your study to other Super Series workbooks covering related or different subject areas, you will find a comprehensive list at the back of this book.

2 Links to ILM qualifications

This workbook relates to the following learning outcomes in segments from the Institute of Leadership & Management (ILM) Level 3 Introductory Certificate in First Line Management and the Level 3 Certificate in First Line Management.

C7.2 Delegation
1 Understand power and authority, responsibility and accountability within an organization
2 Understand the process of effective delegation and its role in empowering staff
3 Recognize and encourage commitment and participation
4 Encourage and support individuals to accept responsibility
5 Monitor progress
6 Provide constructive feedback

Workbook introduction

3 Links to S/NVQs in Management

This workbook relates to the following elements of the Management Standards, which are used in S/NVQs in Management, as well as a range of other S/NVQs.

Unit C12 Lead the work of teams and individuals to achieve objectives

    C12.1   Plan the work of teams and individuals
    C12.2   Assess the work of teams and individuals
    C12.3   Provide feedback to teams and individuals on their work

It will also help you to develop the following Personal Competences:

- acting assertively;
- building teams;
- communicating;
- thinking and taking decisions.

4 Workbook objectives

What happens to the work in your section when you aren't there? Does the work still get done, or does it just stumble along until you get back? Many first line managers and team leaders report that there is usually a huge backlog of questions and problems waiting for them as soon as they walk through the door.

On one level this can be a great comfort – showing, as it does, just how important the manager is to the work of his or her section. But you probably agree that such dependence can put enormous pressures on any manager. It also suggests that the manager's team is not working together effectively, and perhaps that the manager is not developing the overall competence of the team. But one of the major responsibilities of managers is to build a team which can get the work done efficiently and effectively.

Workbook introduction

Delegation allows you to share some of your work and responsibilities with your team members, and it is an important skill for managing, organizing and developing your team.

In this workbook we will be exploring what delegation means, why it is important and what it involves. We will look at the advantages of delegating work, why some managers are reluctant to delegate and at how to achieve a balance when you delegate. Then we will turn to the question of how to delegate successfully. We will investigate such issues as:

- what tasks can be delegated;
- to whom we should delegate;
- how to set objectives for a delegated task;
- how to brief a team member for delegation;
- what controls we need to use.

The workbook helps you to put effective delegation into practice in your own work.

4.1 Objectives

When you have worked through this workbook you will **be better able to**:

- explain why delegation is an important management technique;
- achieve a balance in the extent to which you delegate;
- use the process of delegation to delegate effectively;
- control your workteam more efficiently.

5 Activity planner

The following Activities require some planning so you may want to look at these now.

Activity 20 asks you to draw up a work diary so you can get a clear idea of what you actually do during the day, rather than what you think or plan to spend your time doing.

Activities 22, 23, 24, 26, 28, 29, 30, 31, 32, 34 and 35 are a series of 11 Activities which guide you through the process of effective delegation.

Workbook introduction

Some or all of these Activities may provide the basis of evidence for your S/NVQ portfolio. All Portfolio Activities and the Work-based assignment are signposted with this icon.

The icon states the elements to which the Portfolio Activities and Work-based assignment relate.

Session A
Delegation – a vital skill

1 Introduction

Effective delegation enables you to get work done through other people and is central to effective management.

In recent years we have seen changes in the way work is organized. Organizations and workteams have become 'lean', but a lean workteam is no use unless it is flexible and able to respond quickly to new circumstances. So it is athletic workteams we need, not skeletons! Being flexible means being capable of being deployed where you are most needed. Delegating to your team means that you build up a pool of experience and skill which you can use in a flexible way. It also enables you to cope with pressure at work, when your organization asks you to achieve more in your work.

In this session we'll look at what is involved in delegating, and we will demonstrate that its practice is a skill, and as such can be both learned and improved.

Poorly managed delegation can lead people to think that delegation means someone is 'passing the buck', or just getting someone else to do their work for them. We'll see why effective delegation could not be further from this dismissive description. We'll show how it is an important technique to use for managing your team successfully.

Session A

2 What does delegation mean?

Giving a definition of delegation may seem a bit like trying to define 'electricity'. Although it is fairly easy to see what it can do for you, it is difficult to describe what it is in words. Still, we need to start this session by knowing and agreeing what we are talking about. So what does delegation mean to you?

Activity 1 · 5 mins

Spend a little time thinking about delegation, perhaps your experience of delegation or delegation that you have observed at work. Then write down in a few lines what you think it means.

_____

_____

_____

We have already said that some people regard delegation as passing the buck, but let's hope you have found a more positive description.

I would define delegation in the following way.

- Delegation means giving someone else the responsibility and authority to act on your behalf.

You may have used different words in your description and still be correct. The important words are **responsibility** and **authority** and we will come back to these later.

So, if you delegate, you ask somebody else to **do** something or to make something happen, much as you normally do in your job.

Session A

You will know from your own experience that to make something happen at work you need resources of some kind. If you delegate a certain responsibility, then the member of your team who takes on that responsibility will need resources too, and you will have to think through how they are to be allocated.

Activity 2

5 mins

What are the resources which a manager has to allocate? List at least three in the space below.

_____

_____

_____

Which of these do you think is the most important?

_____

I hope we can agree that the resources which managers can allocate include equipment and materials, finance, information, time and people.

In most situations, people are the most important resource. People bring their skills and expertise to act on other resources in order to achieve results. Without their co-operation nothing will happen.

So delegation means negotiating agreement with other people in order to:

- give them **responsibility** to act on your behalf;
- give them the **authority** needed to get the job done;
- allocate **resources** to them – including other people – that are needed to get the job done.

3 Why is it important to delegate?

As a first line manager your organization has given you the authority to use resources to achieve results. For example, you use information from team

Session A

members and from senior managers to make decisions and take action. You can share some of this authority with team members so they too can achieve results.

Delegating responsibility to team members can be one of the most helpful things you can do for them.

Effective delegation benefits team members in the following ways.

- Delegation helps people to develop new skills and competence and so demonstrate their ability.
- It helps people become more involved and trusted at work and to feel that they are valued members of the team.
- It gives people a wider and more varied experience at work than they might otherwise get.
- It enables people to find out more about what is going on.
- It helps staff to feel empowered and increases their commitment.

> 'True delegation, effective delegation, is delegation with trust and with only the necessary minimum of controls.'
>
> Charles Handy
> *Understanding Organizations*
> (1999, p. 284).

Successful delegation helps to **develop** team members who are competent, involved, committed and well-informed. Such team members are likely to perform highly – a real asset to any organization.

By using delegation to help their team members, managers are also helping themselves – for you'll probably agree it is easier to work with a well-motivated competent team, than with a group of people who are reluctant to do the work and are not interested in what they are doing.

But delegation is also an important management technique for at least four other reasons. It helps managers to:

- make better decisions;
- make the most of their own limited time;
- keep control of a large team;
- improve the team's overall performance.

Let's look at these in turn.

3.1 Making better decisions

As a team leader your role is to manage your team and the work it does. To do so effectively you need to make good decisions about all aspects of the work of the team.

Session A

Activity 3

3 mins

What do think is needed if good decisions are to be made?

_____

_____

You may have mentioned the importance of reliable, up-to-date and complete information. I would argue that you need to have access to quality information in order to make a good decision.

As a team leader you are at the centre of a network of communications with information flowing from you and to you in all directions (see diagram). Your management perspective gives you an overview of what is going on – something which possibly none of your workteam quite shares. The better the flow of information, the better you can plan, organize and control the work for which you are responsible.

```
                    Passes relevant          Receives information
                    information to managers  and instructions
                                             from managers
    Receives                                                          Passes
    information                                                       information
    from other                                                        to other
    team leaders    ───────►   ┌─────────────┐   ───────►              team leaders
    and different              │ Team leader │                         in other parts of
    parts of the               └─────────────┘                         the workplace
    workplace
                    Receives information     Gives information
                    from the workteam        and instructions
                                             to workteam
```

> 'All decisions should be made as low as possible in the organization. The Charge of the Light Brigade was ordered by an officer who wasn't there looking at the territory.'
>
> Robert Townsend, author of *Up the Organization*.

But even in the best-run teams there are bound to be gaps in the team leader's store of information. In fact, the more teams are encouraged to take responsibility for their own work, to develop their own skills and to take a real interest in all aspects of the job, the greater becomes the detailed information and knowledge available within the team and the smaller the proportion of it that the team leader will know. It is simply a fact of life that the team leader is not going to know everything. Part of the reason for this is that detailed knowledge comes with actually doing the job and that is not what team leaders are usually paid for. Their job is to get the job done through other people.

Delegation is a way of tapping into the detailed knowledge and information within your team and bringing these to bear upon specific tasks or projects. By encouraging your team to contribute the detailed information you may

Session A

well lack, you will have more confidence that your management decisions are sound. Greater participation by staff can be a real source of solid support on a day-to-day basis.

3.2 Effective use of limited time

Most managers have more work to do than they have time for, and very often feel that some of their work never gets done or doesn't get the attention it deserves. Delegation allows managers to balance their workload.

- Managers can delegate the low to medium priority jobs to others and, by doing so, make sure that the jobs get done properly.
- With the time saved by giving some of their work to others, they will have more time to work on the high priority jobs and the work which only they can do.

Although the process of delegation takes time, bear in mind that it is time spent **developing team members and giving them an opportunity to grow**. This is an important management responsibility. So delegation represents effective use of a manager's time.

3.3 Keeping control

'Span of control' is a term used to describe the number of members in a workteam for which a particular manager is responsible. That is, it states the number of people under their control.

We'll look at what this means in practice.

Activity 4

5 mins

Alex works for a large insurance company and is responsible for a sales team of forty. Recently the company brought in a new bonus scheme linked to the amount of new work each salesperson obtained. This resulted in the sales team increasing their individual business by an average of 25%. As a consequence, Alex's own workload increased considerably and the office work has begun to get into a bit of a mess.

Session A

Alex was called into the sales manager's office and asked to explain why things had got out of control lately. The manager suggested that Alex needed to take a course in office management so as to be better able to cope with the work. Alex's response to this was to say that what was needed was not more training but fewer people to supervise.

Which of these two suggestions do you think is more likely to solve Alex's problem?

_____

_____

I expect you agree that Alex's problem is not likely to be a lack of training, but too large a span of control. It is always going to be difficult to control a team of forty without having assistance.

There is no definite 'best' number of people that a first line manager can control, but some management experts have suggested that it can be as high as twelve, provided these people do not themselves supervise others. Much depends on the circumstances, such as the nature of the job, the time available for direct supervision, the character of the workteam and the amount of training received.

What is clear is that the greater the number of people in a workteam, the more difficult it is for their manager to keep control.

Delegation is a major way of coping with a large a span of control, and it is the reason why organizations use 'family-tree'-type structures, that look like this.

```
                    ┌─────────────────┐
                    │ Senior manager  │
                    └────────┬────────┘
           ┌─────────────────┼─────────────────┐
    ┌──────┴──────┐   ┌──────┴──────┐   ┌──────┴──────┐
    │ Team leader │   │ Team leader │   │ Team leader │
    └──────┬──────┘   └──────┬──────┘   └──────┬──────┘
      │││││││             │││││││            │││││││
    Team members       Team members        Team members
```

The workforce is divided into teams, usually with a team leader or first line manager responsible for a relatively small number of people.

Delegating work is one important way to help you keep effective control of a large group of people. By using delegation, you can give each member of

Session A

your workteam responsibility for making sure their own part of the group's work fits into place. This encourages greater commitment and participation, essential elements of successful teamwork.

In this way a workteam is rather like an orchestra – each section, such as the strings, percussion, and so on, is responsible for its own part of the musical score – with you playing the role of conductor and being responsible for bringing all the parts together for a perfect performance.

3.4 Improving the team's performance

> 'Management, above everything else, is about people. It is about the accomplishment of ends and aims by the efforts of groups of people working together.'
>
> Sir John Harvey-Jones.

To improve the way your team works you need to bring together the individual contributions of the people in your workteam so that they form a united group, working towards the same ends. This involves:

- getting to know each team member – their strengths and weaknesses, their personal aims and ambitions, what aspects of their work they enjoy and dislike and so on;
- making sure the goals and objectives of the team are understood and shared by everyone;
- planning to make the best use of each team member so that everyone is fully committed to the team effort.

Activity 5 · 5 mins

How do you think delegating work can actually improve team performance?

_____
_____
_____
_____

Delegation gives you the opportunity to make the most of the individuals in your team and to show that you value them and their work. You can improve the team's performance by delegating in two different ways.

Session A

EXTENSION 1
As a team leader you need to motivate your team members. To find out more about motivation, see Extension 1 on page 93.

- You can **build on the strengths of each team member**. If one person is better at a certain type of work than others, it makes sense to use that strength by delegating that particular job to him or her. In this way you improve the team's commitment.
- On the other hand you may plan to use delegation to **develop the skills of an individual team member**. Here you are demonstrating confidence that the individual has the potential to develop new skills, thus increasing their opportunities to particpate, and you are working to improve the pool of skills in the team.

Activity 6 — 10 mins

Think about what you have learned about the importance of delegating, and give at least one reason why delegating is important to the following people.

- Team leaders.

- Team members.

- Organizations.

With effective delegation, everybody wins.

Delegation enables team leaders to:

- develop a committed and motivated team;
- develop the skills of individuals;
- draw on the expertise of their team members;
- make better decisions;
- make effective use of their own time;
- co-ordinate and control a team;
- improve the performance of the team.

9

Session A

Effective delegation can help individual team members to:

- increase their skills and expertise;
- get a variety of experience, increasing their opportunities to participate;
- feel that they are trusted and valued members of the team, which encourages greater commitment;
- increase their knowledge about the organization and the work of the team as a whole.

Delegation can promote a competent, committed, enthusiastic and well-informed workforce, and this is obviously important to any organization. But delegation is also important to organizations because it increases the flow of information at all levels, and effective communications throughout an organization are essential for good decision-making.

4 Objections to delegating

We have seen some of the main reasons why delegation is an important technique, bringing benefits to team members, team leaders and the organization as a whole.

But some team leaders seem to be rather reluctant to pass on work to members of their workteam.

Activity 7 · 3 mins

Jot down one or two reasons for reluctance to delegate work.

_____
_____
_____
_____

Session A

You could have thought of a number of possibilities. The first ones that strike me are the following.

- People may think that it's quicker to do the job themselves, or find that they are not satisfied with the quality of job that one of their workteam would do, and so prefer to do the job themselves.
- As we have already mentioned, delegation demands that you make resources available, and in an attempt to protect their position of authority, some people like to keep resources – especially information – to themselves.
- People may feel that asking somebody else to do something implies that they are not able to do it themselves and are not really up to the job.
- They may not trust the workteam and may feel that delegation of work means it is going outside their control.

Although we may recognize these concerns, we will see in this workbook that they do not represent sound reasons for reluctance to delegate. They suggest, instead, a misunderstanding about what delegation actually involves. We'll look at this in some detail, but first let's return to the ideas of authority and responsibility that are at the core of delegating.

5 Authority and responsibility

We have already suggested that delegation happens when, as a team leader, you negotiate with a member of your workteam to give them the authority to do something on your behalf. At the same time, you have made them **responsible** for doing the job.

However, this doesn't mean that you can pass responsibility to them for seeing that the job gets done properly, and on time.

If you give a team member the **authority** to do something, you may be losing some authority, since you no longer make the decisions – they are made by the team member instead. But when you give authority to the team member, you do not lose any **responsibility** – if anything you increase it. Although the team member is responsible for doing the job, you are responsible both for getting it done and for trusting the team member to do it. So delegation means you **lose** some authority, but both you and the team member **gain** responsibility.

In the end the **overall responsibility** is yours – after all, that's what managers and team leaders are paid for. Otherwise you have given up your job altogether, rather than just delegating a part of it.

Session A

5.1 Responsibility and accountability

These terms are often used interchangeably, but in fact they mean different things. It helps to think of them as 'responsibility for' and 'accountability to' in order to perceive the distinction. As we've seen, there are things about your job that you are always responsible for, including the outcome of the delegated tasks. However, your job in the organization's hierarchy inevitably means that you are **accountable to** or **answerable to** someone else higher up the line of authority. This is why you can never relinquish ultimate responsibility, because it is you who will have to answer for the consequences of any actions that you take.

> Who are you accountable to in your organization? And who is accountable to you?

> Peter was managing a large publishing project for a client. The workload turned out to be much heavier than he had anticipated, and in order to meet the deadline, he sub-contracted part of the work to another freelance colleague, Gerry. Despite Peter's careful instructions, Gerry made what Peter described as 'a complete pig's ear' of the job. 'It just wasn't possible to send the work back to the client,' he said to a friend. 'They would have just flung it back in my face. And you can't say, "Well, it's not my fault, someone else made a mess of it." It was up to me to make sure it was sent off to the client in an acceptable state. So I worked day and night for several days to make sure it was. It was me who would have to explain to the client why the work was in a mess, not Gerry, because I was ultimately responsible for the job, not him.'

5.2 Authority and power

Authority also gives power. Your authority as a manager gives you power to influence other people. One definition of power is 'the means of influencing the thoughts and actions of others'. The higher up the organization people are, the more power and influence they have. This is **position power**, and we'll look at it briefly here. Your job as a manager gives you position power.

There are different degrees of position power, depending on how high up you are in the organization. The managing director will have a great deal more position power than a first line manager. He or she will be able to influence many more people's thoughts and actions and to a much greater extent.

There are various strategies you can employ as a supervisor to influence your staff. Some will be particularly effective when your position power is high. Others will depend more on using **personal power**. These strategies include:

Session A

- **assertiveness** – used most frequently when position power is high but success will be difficult to achieve;
- **friendliness** – often used when both position power and expectations of success are low;
- **reason** – used frequently when position power and expectations of success are high;
- **referral** to a higher authority;
- **sanctions** or **disciplinary action**.

You'll often use more than one strategy, but you should aim to avoid using the last two unless absolutely necessary.

> Deena had been recently promoted to a managerial position. At first she felt uncomfortable in the role because she was no longer at the same level as her colleagues, with whom she'd been very friendly, and she felt they no longer regarded her in the same way as before. She tried adopting the strategy of asking them to do things in a friendly way. Although this worked part of the time, if it was a case of asking someone to do an unpopular task, it was more difficult to get anyone to agree. They'd make a joke of it and make excuses as to why they couldn't do it, and she spent a lot of time trying to persuade people to no avail. Eventually Deena went on an assertiveness training course, and now has a much better idea of how to use her personal power in an assertive way to get things done.

If you are interested in learning more about the issues of authority and power, responsibility and accountability, you might like to study the workbook *Managing Relationships at Work* in this series.

Activity 8

5 mins

Jot down what you see as the difference in the responsibility for a job between a team leader and a member of their workteam to whom they have delegated it.

Session A

> Richard E. Krafve, President of Raytheon Corporation put the issue of authority and responsibility succinctly.
>
> 'You can delegate authority, but you can never delegate responsibility by delegating a task to someone else.'

I hope you agree that the difference is that the workteam member has the responsibility for doing the job, but that the team leader is responsible for seeing that it gets done, properly and on time.

In other words, as a team leader, you must stay in overall **control** of the work.

If you delegate effectively, you will stay in overall control. Let's see what's involved in effective delegation.

6 The process of delegation

To delegate effectively you need to take time to prepare to delegate and then go on to carry out the delegation.

Preparing to delegate
- Decide what to delegate
- Select team members

Carrying out the delegation
- Set objectives
- Plan
- Implement
- Monitor
- Review

Session A

In **preparing to delegate** you look at the overall picture of your work, and the workload, competence and needs of team members. You will decide:

- what tasks, activities and duties you can delegate;
- to which of your team members you delegate these to.

We look at preparing to delegate in Session C.

To carry out the delegation you need to do the following.

- **Set and agree the objectives**. In other words, what do you want the person to whom you are delegating to achieve?

- **Plan** the delegation by:
  - allocating appropriate resources – in other words, what resources are needed to achieve the objectives, including support from you;
  - deciding how to keep track of progress – for example, at what stages will the person taking on the task report to you;
  - briefing the team member and agreeing the way forward, and agreeing milestones, in other words what will be achieved when.

- **Let the team member implement** the delegated task – when the team member begins to do the work, you take a back seat while still providing support and controlling the work in the ways you have agreed.

- **Monitor** the delegated task – both you and the person carrying out the delegation will need to keep an eye on progress, to ensure the task is going according to plan and going to meet the objectives, and then taking action, where appropriate to ensure the task stays on course.

- **Review** the delegated task with the team member when it is completed by:
  - evaluating what went well and what aspects could be improved next time;
  - giving helpful feedback to the team member to improve future performance.

Notice that these stages – setting objectives, planning, implementing, monitoring and reviewing – tend to form a continuous cycle. This is because when you have completed the review stage you are then ready to set new or revised objectives. As a team leader you may be familiar with this cycle which is used for planning and controlling many work activities.

We will look in more detail at the stages of carrying out the delegation in Session D.

Session A

Activity 9

5 mins

You have looked briefly at what's involved in delegating effectively. Write a checklist of the things team leaders must do to meet their responsibilities when delegating tasks to their team. We have given the first one to start you off.

When delegating team leaders need to:

- decide which of their tasks they can delegate;

Your checklist should show that team leaders need to prepare for delegating by deciding what to delegate and who to delegate to. They then need to set objectives and plan the delegation. They need to support the team member who is carrying out the delegated task and monitor the task in the ways that have been agreed. Finally they need to review the delegation with the team member, providing appropriate feedback and considering how to make improvements next time. By using the process of delegation, team leaders meet their responsibilities for getting the job done properly.

7 How effective delegation will help you

We have seen that with delegation everybody wins, and we have looked at the stages involved in delegating effectively. Before we look at the particular advantages you are likely to gain from effective delegation, work through the next activity.

Session A

Activity 10

15 mins

Answer Yes or No to each of the following questions.

1 Do you spend time doing things which you think other people in your workteam could do for you?   YES / NO

2 Do you find that a number of tasks on your list of jobs cannot be placed under the headings of planning, organizing, motivating, developing or controlling, creating and communicating?   YES / NO

3 Do you work on jobs which you like to do, although others in your workteam could do them just as well, if not better?   YES / NO

4 Do you find yourself frequently interrupted by telephone calls which could just as easily be dealt with by someone else?   YES / NO

5 If you are temporarily away from your workteam, do they have to delay decisions until you come back?   YES / NO

6 Do you find that others seldom reach the high standards you set for them?   YES / NO

7 At the end of the day, do you have a number of unfinished tasks which you feel should have been done?   YES / NO

8 Is it difficult for you to find time to consult with your workteam regularly?   YES / NO

9 Do you keep information about work tasks to yourself on the grounds that, as supervisor, you ought to know things the rest of your team don't need to know?   YES / NO

10 Do you feel that in general you are overworked?   YES / NO

11 Do you have problems with access to the information or contacts you need to make decisions?   YES / NO

12 Are you slowed down by the lack of authority to make decisions?   YES / NO

Session A

The answers you have given to questions 1–10 should help you to make your own case for delegating effectively. They should show you what advantages you might gain from delegating to your workteam.

> Think about the advantages which you most want to gain from delegating. You will need to identify these for your personal development plan.

If you answered 'Yes' to either question 11 or 12, you need to ask yourself 'Is it within my knowledge and authority to do this?' If your answer is 'No', then you may have a case for upward delegation. So far we have tended to look at delegation in terms of the tasks and responsibilities you delegate to your team. But when you think about your team, you should also include your own line manager. It may simply be more effective occasionally to pass a specific task upwards than to attempt to do it yourself or pass it downwards.

To gain advantages from delegation – whether down to your team or upwards to your line manager – you must become an effective delegator. We will look at the skills involved in delegating in the next sessions, and you will have an opportunity to practise using these skills in your workplace.

In this session we have looked at the meaning of delegation, and at the reasons why it is important to delegate to your team. We have introduced the process of effective delegation, which involves preparing for the delegation – deciding what and to whom to delegate and then carrying it out through the activities of setting objectives, planning, implementing, monitoring and reviewing. You have looked at your own situation, and at how delegating could benefit you. By now you should have an idea of the advantages you want to gain through effective delegation.

In the next session we look at how to find a balance in delegating.

Self-assessment 1

20 mins

For questions 1 to 6 complete the sentences with a suitable word or words.

1 Delegation means giving someone _____ and _____ to act on your behalf.

2 If a task is delegated to you, you also need _____ allocated to you in order to carry it out.

3 When you delegate a task, you have _____ _____ for seeing that a job is done properly and on time.

Session A

4 Successful delegation helps to develop team members who are _____, _____, _____ and _____.

5 Delegation enables team leaders to draw on the expertise of team members and so improve _____-_____.

6 Give two reasons why delegating represents an effective use of your time.

_____

_____

_____

_____

7 What does 'span of control' mean?

_____

_____

8 Complete the following diagram to show the process of delegation.

Answers to these questions can be found on page 95.

19

Session A

8 Summary

- Delegation means giving someone else the **responsibility** to act for you and the **authority** to do it.

- **Authority** confers **power**, which may in practice flow from the position (position power) or from the person who holds it (personal power).

- Delegation helps to make team members well-informed **participants**, who are competent, involved and **committed**.

- **Delegation** is an important management technique to use to:
  - make better decisions;
  - make effective use of time;
  - keep control of a large team;
  - improve the performance of the team.

- The ultimate responsibility for seeing that a job is done properly and on time is the team leader's.

- Managers are **responsible for** the tasks and the people over whom they have authority; they are **accountable to** the person in authority over them.

- To keep **control** of a delegated task you need to delegate effectively as follows.
  - **Prepare** for delegation by choosing an appropriate task and selecting an appropriate person.
  - **Carry out** the delegation by:
    setting clear objectives;
    planning;
    implementing;
    monitoring;
    reviewing.
  - **Review the delegation.**

Session B
Achieving balance in delegation

1 Introduction

To get the most benefit from delegation, you have to get the balance just right. Too little, or under-delegation, suggests a lack of trust and confidence. Too much, or over-delegation, suggests a loss of control.

In this session we'll look at some of the reasons why people do not always get it right. We shall look at both under-delegation and over-delegation, and put them in the context of what happens in an actual workplace. Then we will look at the levels of control in effective delegation.

2 Under-delegation

Under-delegation comes about if you fail to pass enough responsibility down the line to your workteam, and try to do too much yourself instead.

> Susan Ward, a receptionist in a health clinic, was discussing with her colleagues a new way of index-filing which her office manager had introduced. 'It's a total disaster.' she said. 'We can't find anything these days without going through every file. Mind you, I knew it wouldn't

Session B

> work when she told me about it, but I didn't bother telling her. After all my job is only to do as I'm told, isn't it? It's management's job to tell us what to do, and then they're carrying the can if anything goes wrong. After all, that's what they get paid for.'

This case shows a mistake often made by managers. They are not necessarily in the best position to decide about changes in working methods.

Those who are closest to the work, as in this case Susan herself, are more likely to know what is suitable and what is not. So enabling the workteam to participate in deciding what is to be done helps you to make better decisions. It also helps to build up a good team spirit. In the end, we have to rely to a large extent on the good relationship we have with our workteam in order to bring in new methods without too much fuss.

You will probably agree that Susan's reference to her manager as 'she' suggests that there isn't much of a team spirit in their office.

> At the supervisors' weekly meeting, George Reynolds was describing to the others some of the problems he was having with his workteam. 'If I want a job done properly I have to do it myself,' he said, 'and if I'm not around, then nothing gets done.' Ravi Patel, another of the supervisors, suggested to George that he should involve his workteam more in making decisions about their work, and should delegate some responsibility to them so that they could act on their own. 'By doing this, I find my team feel responsible for what gets done and they are both willing and able to do jobs which otherwise I would have to do myself,' said Ravi.

I expect you agree that Ravi is right in the way he involves his workteam. The advantages to him are that his team is able to carry on without his direct supervision, because they can make decisions and have a good team spirit, which makes them more committed to doing the job.

2.1 Reasons for under-delegating

Some managers say they would like to delegate, but they just can't fit it into their work schedules. They feel it is quicker to do the job themselves than to explain it to other people. Delegating does take time to plan and organize. But by delegating some of their work, managers will have more time to

Session B

concentrate on the important work of managing. It is also worth bearing in mind that by going through the process of delegating you are actually carrying out some of your duties for developing your workteam.

Some managers take the view that their workteam need to be told what to do and that they will avoid work if they can. They feel that they can do the job better than any member of their staff.

This seems rather like parents always tying their children's shoelaces for them, rather than showing them how to do it and then waiting while they struggle to do it for themselves. If you never let people learn to do things for themselves, they will never be independent.

On the other hand, if you consider your workteam to be a highly skilled and very capable group, and then act accordingly, your own position is raised in status.

In other words, showing a willingness to delegate suggests confidence both in your workteam to accept responsibility and in your own ability to manage.

Managers who hesitate to delegate often do so because they believe it will enhance their own reputation if they do the job themselves. In fact, the opposite is true. A reluctance to delegate is likely to reduce a manager's reputation in other people's eyes, but the ability to do so effectively will raise it.

Thinking that delegating work to others suggests a lack of ability to do it yourself is the result of feeling insecure. Keeping things to yourself because you think that only by knowing things others don't can you keep control, is also a sign of insecurity. Insecure managers fear that passing on part of their job to someone else means that they will no longer be needed themselves.

However, you have to be realistic about the extent of your authority and your access to information and other resources. You may be able to perform more effectively by involving your manager in a particular stage of a job. This will not undermine your position, but it will enable you to achieve better results.

Insecure managers are prey to upward delegation, where members of the workteam bring a job to their manager and succeed in getting it done for them. It can be flattering when someone says to you, 'I've got this job to do, but I've come to you with it because I know you can do it much better than me.' However, it can sometimes be dangerous to accept the job.

Session B

Activity 11

5 mins

What do you think are the dangers of allowing a team member to delegate work up to the manager? Note at least one danger here.

_____

_____

_____

There are several dangers in this situation.

- If you spend time and energy doing the work of your team member you cannot be properly doing your own.
- You may be making 'a rod for your own back', since if you allow it to happen once, it is likely that you will be asked to do it again.
- You are not in control of your workteam if you allow a team member to dictate what you should do.
- You are likely to believe that your team member is less capable than you previously thought.

If you treat your workteam as incompetent, and do everything for them, they will come to expect this and won't accept responsibility for themselves.

> Do you believe in self-fulfilling prophecies? In other words, if you expect people to be incompetent do you think they are likely to be incompetent?

However, on occasions, your team members will legitimately delegate upwards to you. You should expect and encourage team members to pass on to you:

- those aspects of work which you have the knowledge, information and contacts to do more effectively because of your management position;
- decisions which they do not have the authority or responsibility to make, for example, the responsibility to discipline somebody or to access restricted information.

> A number of manufacturing companies spotted the following effect in quality control. At one time quality was the responsibility of a specialist inspection department. Production workers were not responsible for checking the quality of their own work since this was the job of an inspector. This arrangement often led to competition developing between production and inspection departments, with production blaming any low productivity on inspection's lack of co-operation.

Session B

Many companies changed this system, so that production workers are now responsible for checking their own work and making sure it is up to standard. This has led to improvements in quality, with improved productivity and less re-work. By delegating to all workers responsibility for their own work, they improved standards of work and proved the competence of their workforce.

A final reason for a reluctance to delegate is when managers are so keen to do the work themselves, they do not want to let someone else share in it.

This can be particularly true of a manager who has come up 'through the ranks' – that is, someone responsible for others doing work which he or she used to do. In this case, the manager often prefers doing the job, rather than doing management work – perhaps because of a lack of confidence in his or her ability to manage. However, managers have to learn to let go of their old job in order to have time to be effective in their new role.

Activity 12

10 mins

Imagine you are in a team leaders' team meeting. The team leaders give four different reasons why they tend not to delegate. For each reason given below, suggest an argument you would use to persuade the team leaders that delegation will help them.

Reason	How delegating can help
Lack of time for delegating.	_____
Lack of confidence in the abilities of team members.	_____

25

Session B

Fear of losing their reputation by sharing their workload.

Easier to do the work themselves than to delegate it.

Your answers may be slightly different from the following ones, but they should be along the same lines.

Reason	How delegation can help
Lack of time for delegating	Although it takes time, delegation gives you more time to concentrate on the important work of managing.
Lack of confidence in the abilities of team members	You can use delegation as a development activity. By reviewing how well someone has performed and then giving them slightly more responsibility next time, you will increase confidence and trust between you.
Fear of losing their reputation by sharing their workload	You are more likely to lose your reputation if you keep your work to yourself. A competent, successful team reflects well on you, and enhances your reputation. You can develop a successful team by delegating.
Easier to do the work themselves than to delegate it	This puts a lot of pressure on you; and what happens when you aren't there? As a team leader you need to work to develop your team and increase their skills, and delegating part of your work is one way of doing this.

Do you think you under-delegate? If you recognize any of the reasons for under-delegating here, you may find it helpful to think back to Session A to identify how delegation can actually help you.

26

Session B

3 Over-delegation

Having looked at under-delegation, now let's look at things from the other end: that is, **over-delegation**. This is when too much responsibility is delegated.

Over-delegation occurs when a manager passes on responsibility to other people and fails to control the task that has been delegated. If a manager is delegating a lot of work to a number of different people, but is still retaining control over the work, then he or she is not over-delegating.

There are several explanations for over-delegating. Some managers find that they have given away too many tasks to too many people, and find they have over-delegated because they can't keep track of all the work. This can happen quite by accident.

Other managers over-delegate because they are worried by the responsibilities of the job.

> In a large water company it was well known among staff that promotion was mostly for those who did not make mistakes. As a result, acting on their own initiative was avoided by most managers and they tried hard either to make no decisions at all, or else to pass the responsibility for making them to other members of their workteam. In this way, they felt someone else would be 'carrying the can' if something went wrong.

Perhaps you'll agree that the company needs to change the image of its promotion policy. However, although the managers are trying to avoid their responsibilities they will find that it is impossible to do so. When something goes wrong, then a workteam member delegated to make a decision will swiftly pass any blame straight back to the manager – where it belongs.

You may also find that some managers over-delegate in order to avoid conflict.

Session B

Activity 13

6 mins

> Carla Franklin has just been appointed manager of the electrical department of a major department store. She has previously worked in several different departments in the store since leaving school six years ago, but never before in electrical. The most experienced member of the electrical department is Brian Haynes, who has worked in it for the last twenty years, and who really thought he would get the manager's job when it became vacant. In order to avoid possible conflict, Carla has decided to let Brian take on a large part of the responsibility for the day-to-day management of the department and to deal with all representatives of suppliers to the store.

What problems is Carla creating for herself by delegating in this way?

_____
_____
_____

I think you would probably agree that this arrangement may help to prevent conflict in the beginning between Carla and Brian. But it looks as though Carla is avoiding her own responsibilities. By delegating in this way, there is a danger that the rest of the team will accept Brian as the 'real' manager. This is bound to lead to conflict in the end.

If Carla has a problem with the electrical side, then one solution is to delegate that aspect, but to sit in on meetings to learn the ropes, and to take part in planning and controlling the work. Another solution is for Carla to go on a suitable course.

Another reason why managers over-delegate is through lack of motivation.

Session B

Activity 14

7 mins

Think for a moment about the factors at work which motivate you: that is, those things which encourage you to keep on working.

Jot down **two** or **three** of them.

_____
_____
_____

Your answers will be particular to you.

Management experts find it hard to pin down the factors that lead people to feel motivated to work. Surprisingly, perhaps, they have found that being paid is not a sufficient motivator by itself. They have identified a range of factors to do with the job itself which can lead to motivation. For example, people are likely to feel motivated if they find their work interesting, if they like the people they work with, or work for a good employer who considers their needs and tries to allow for them. The way people are treated by their manager is also likely to affect the extent to which people feel motivated.

People who don't enjoy their work, who feel their employer disregards them and who do not have a supportive or encouraging manager are unlikely to be motivated to work. Their lack of enthusiasm may lead them to try to shed their work through over-delegating.

Perhaps the best way to tell if someone is over-delegating is to consider whether he or she still has control over the work being done.

4 Identifying under-delegation and over-delegation

Think about managers you know, or have known, at your workplace and the ways in which they have delegated jobs to members of their team.

Session B

Activity 15

15 mins

Who has tended to either under-delegate or over-delegate to others? Why do you think this has been the case, and what do you feel have been the results of their actions? Write your ideas below.

Under/over-delegation	Reason	Effects

Compare the reasons you have written down with those that we have suggested for under-delegation or over-delegation. You may agree that the effects of under-delegation include:

- a feeling of 'them' and 'us' among the workteam;
- the manager feels overworked and is not able to give time to managing the team;
- team members cannot actively participate;
- a lack of team spirit among the team.

You may agree that the effects of over-delegation include the following:

- the manager loses control of the workteam;
- the authority of the manager is undermined;
- there is little unity in the workteam.

If you feel that you either under-delegate or over-delegate, you may need to find a balance between trust and control in the way you delegate.

Session B

5 Levels of control in delegation

We have seen that in delegating effectively you will stay in overall control. However, as a manager you can choose an appropriate level of control to match:

- your preferred approach;
- the skills, experience and attitudes of your team members;
- the constraints of the job.

In general, the level of control managers use in delegation will relate to the extent to which they trust their team members to do a good job. You can see the relationship between trust and control in this graph.

Managers who have a high degree of trust in team members are likely to feel they need to take little direct control of the work themselves.

For example, when a manager gives a team member a high level of responsibility for the delegated task, the team member is able to make his or

31

Session B

her own decisions as to method, timing, resources and so on, although he or she will usually discuss these decisions with the manager, and the manager may offer guidance, advice and support.

Here is how one manager explains how she controls her team.

> 'I find the best way to keep things under control is to make sure my team know what we need to achieve and the importance of working to company regulations and procedures. I make sure they know they can come to me to discuss ideas and explore possibilities. Then I leave them to carry on with the job, only checking that it is going OK in an informal way.'

When managers have a low level of confidence or trust in team members they are likely to take a high level of direct control of the work, and limit the responsibility they give to each person. For example, they may tell the team member how to do the job, and ask for regular and routine progress reports at various stages.

Whatever level of control is used, it is important to bear in mind that, since nobody is perfect, some mistakes are bound to be made by your team. However, this should not stop you delegating to them.

Activity 16 · 5 mins

How do you feel when someone shows that they trust you to do something on their behalf?

_____

_____

How do you feel when someone asks you to do something, but then doesn't let you get on with it, and clearly doesn't trust you to get it right?

_____

_____

I think most people feel committed to doing a good job when they are entrusted with it. They are likely to put in the effort required to get it right. But when they know they aren't expected to do a good job, most people would lack motivation, commitment and interest in the work.

Session B

Showing you trust your team is important if they are to give their best to a job. However, trust is a quality which grows and develops through experience and over time.

If you do not yet have confidence in team members' abilities, you can use careful delegation to **build trust**. Bear in mind that the process of delegation helps you to develop the skills of your team members.

Use high levels of control when you delegate tasks at first. By doing this, you can give appropriate advice and support whenever you feel the team member needs help. In this way you make it more likely that the team member will succeed. When the team member succeeds in carrying out tasks, you will have more confidence to gradually release direct control, giving that individual more responsibility to do a good job, and showing more trust in them.

Remember that you – as manager – retain overall responsibility for a job you have delegated. In the next two sessions we look at how to do this by going through the process of delegation.

Self-assessment 2

10 mins

1   What are the reasons why a manager might not delegate very much to others? Note down three or four reasons.

a _____

b _____

c _____

d _____

2   Complete the following statement by selecting the best answer out of the three.

A sign that a manager is over-delegating is when he or she:

a   delegates lots of tasks;
b   has no control over the tasks that are delegated;
c   is new to the job.

Session B

3 Complete the following sentence with the appropriate words.

The level of _____ you decide to take when you delegate is related to how much you _____ the person to do a good job.

4 How can you develop trust through delegating?
_____
_____

Answers to these questions can be found on page 96.

6 Summary

- **Under-delegation**, not giving sufficient authority and responsibility to those who work for you, often results in managers:
    - doing too much themselves;
    - being overworked;
    - not using the workteam's expertise in decision-making.

- Managers may under-delegate because:
    - they consider it less bother to do the job themselves;
    - they have too much concern for their own reputation as operators;
    - they lack confidence in their workteam's ability;
    - they feel insecure in their job as a manager;
    - they are too keen to do the operational job themselves.

- **Upward delegation** is when work is passed up to the manager. It may be sensible and more effective to pass work to the manager, especially where more authority is needed to take a decision or do some aspect of a job. However, it is important to ensure that upward delegation is justified.

- **Over-delegation**, passing on too much responsibility to others, can mean the manager loses control of the workteam to someone else.

- Managers may over-delegate because:
    - they lack experience in the job;
    - they are poorly motivated to do their job;
    - they are afraid of making errors themselves.

- The level of direct control you take in delegating is related to the amount of **trust** you have that the person who will carry out the delegated task will do a good job.

- You can develop trust in team members by going carefully through the process of delegation and helping the team member to be successful by using an appropriate level of **control**.

Session C
Preparing to delegate

1 Introduction

In this session and in Session D we examine the process of effective delegation and ask you to apply the process in your work by delegating a suitable task to one of your team members. If you are not yet in a position to delegate, you will still find it useful to work through the sessions now, but plan to work through them again when you come to delegate tasks.

The skills of delegation include knowing what to delegate and to which member of your workteam.

In this session we will look in general terms at what parts of a team leader's job can be delegated; then you will look at your own work to select particular tasks that you can delegate and select a real task which you want to delegate.

Delegation can be a way of demonstrating that you recognize the skills of a particular team member, or the enthusiasm and commitment they possess. Depending on the type of task you delegate, it can also be part of a system of rewards, for example, if you delegate a desirable task rather than one that may be low priority or routine.

The success of delegation depends to a large extent on your choosing the most appropriate person to take on the job. To make this judgement you must get to know the strengths and weaknesses of team members. In the second half of this session you will choose an appropriate team member for the delegated task.

Session C

2 What should not be delegated?

There are clearly parts of any manager's job that cannot be delegated. It is important to identify these activities first and separate them from the others. You can then look at these other jobs and assess which are most suitable for delegating.

Work which is of a confidential nature should not be delegated. Similarly, team leaders cannot delegate tasks for which they do not have the authority in the first place. Nor can they delegate **all** their authority, or they will have passed over the job altogether.

Your company regulations and policies may specify jobs which only you can do, or there may be procedures which only you can undertake.

Activity 17 · 5 mins

Think about your own particular job and write down **two** things which you cannot delegate, and why this is.

_____

_____

Your answers will depend on your own circumstances, but here are some examples of work activities that you would not delegate:

- disciplinary action;
- counselling staff;
- reviewing the performance of team members;
- your role in promoting health and safety at work;
- planning and organizing the work activities of the whole team.

Session C

3 What should be delegated?

We'll now consider which tasks you ought to delegate to your workteam.

Activity 18 · 15 mins

You are the office manager in the editorial department of a publishing company. Much of the work in your department is done by freelance writers, editors, proofreaders, and page designers who work from home. The editorial manager wants to use the regular freelance staff more effectively. By finding out what sort of hardware and software each one uses, the various types of editorial jobs can be distributed more appropriately between them. The editorial manager asks you to do a short survey of the freelance staff, to see what equipment each one has, and which sorts of jobs they feel they are best equipped to do. The editorial manager also wants to increase the pool of design staff, and asks you to draw up a list freelance designers who might be suitable for the company.

You work out that the job involves:

- analysing the different sorts of editorial jobs, and the equipment and software needed for each;
- investigating freelancer editors' equipment and software;
- drawing up a summary of the sorts of editorial jobs each one is best fitted to do;
- deciding what the company's requirements are for freelance designers;
- finding suitable freelance designers;
- pulling all the information together and writing a report.

You are already very busy doing the sort of work that only you can do, and you feel that this project will take up a lot of time that you could use more effectively.

Session C

Which parts of this job would you delegate to someone else, and which would you carry out yourself?

_____
_____
_____
_____
_____
_____

I would suggest that you could delegate to other people in your team:

- the responsibility for analysing the different sorts of jobs, and the equipment and software needed for each;
- surveying freelance editors' equipment and software;
- summarising the sorts of editorial jobs each one is best fitted to do;
- finding freelance designers who are likely to be short-listed.

You might want to check on the company's requirements for designers before someone else does the work of searching for suitable people. In addition, you will probably want to write the final report, although others might also contribute to it. The final decision about which designers might be interviewed is yours, as is the decision about which editorial jobs best suit which freelance editors.

You may have come up with different answers from these, but they are probably based on similar ideas.

You will probably agree that this project would be a useful opportunity for you to work with your workteam and show them that you have confidence in them. The project is interesting and it also enables you to do some work developing your team members. These factors make parts of the project highly suitable for delegation.

The kinds of jobs which are suitable for delegating may include the following:

- jobs which individual team members can do as well as or better than you;
- jobs which serve to develop individuals;
- jobs which are of low to medium priority;
- jobs which are routine;
- jobs which appeal to individual team members.

Let's look at each of these factors in turn.

3.1 Jobs for which team members are competent

As a team leader you need to concentrate on the management activities of planning, organizing, motivating and controlling your workteam. Although you may like to do some of the technical work you were originally trained for, you should bear in mind that your team members are closer to the actual work than you. Therefore, they are likely to have ready access to the information needed to do the job. So you can delegate the parts of a job, often the technical parts, which another member of the workteam can do just as well as, if not better than, you.

For this kind of job you are building on the **existing competence** of team members, making the most of their existing strengths. Indeed, this is an important way of using delegation.

However, you should also consider delegating tasks which will help team members **develop** competence.

3.2 Developmental jobs

As a team leader you have a responsibility to make sure your team members are skilled and experienced to do the work of the team both now and in the future. You also want to build a team that is well-motivated. For this you need to develop individual team members so that they are able to meet current and future demands. Investing in team members through development activities shows that you value their contribution.

Delegation is a valuable technique here. It allows you to share some of your interesting work, and thus show your trust in your team. It is also an effective way of developing people. The work carried out as part of delegation contributes to the work of the section, so is intrinsically useful. But by the end of the delegation process, the team member should have learned new things which he or she can go on to apply and use.

When you identify jobs that will help develop team members, you need to consider whether you can give them access to the resources necessary to do these jobs properly. Although you can allocate many resources, bear in mind that some – for example, information or particular expertise – cannot always be allocated or made easily accessible.

So consider aspects of your work which may be done by a member of your workteam, who would see them as interesting or challenging, a break in their own routine and an opportunity to develop new skills and experience.

Session C

Delegation carried out with these issues in mind can strengthen and empower an individual, because their enthusiasm and commitment have been recognized in a practical way.

3.3 Medium to low priority jobs

Most team leaders have more work to do than they have time for, and so they tend to organize their work according to priority. They focus on jobs which are **urgent** and **important**; in other words high priority jobs. The jobs they leave until last and which may not even get done, are those of lower priority. They may be important, but not urgent, or they may be of relatively low importance. It is these jobs which can be usefully delegated to others.

The chart below shows how jobs may be prioritized according to their importance and urgency, and how far jobs falling into different areas of the chart could be delegated.

```
                          High importance
                                |
     These jobs are             |        Plenty of
     likely to be too           |        scope for
     important and              |        delegating
     urgent for                 |        jobs here
     delegating                 |
                                |
High urgency ───────────────────┼─────────────── Low urgency
                                |
     Too little time            |
     to delegate?               |
                                |        Do these jobs
     Perhaps experienced        |        need to be done
     team members               |        at all?
     could do these jobs        |
                                |
                          Low importance
```

High importance/high urgency Team leaders are likely to want to do these jobs themselves. The jobs have to be done well and they are needed soon, so there is perhaps not enough time to delegate effectively.

High importance/low urgency The jobs in this category will become urgent if they are not done now. They are likely to be suitable for delegating as there is time to plan, monitor and review the job. By delegating relatively important jobs, the team leader is demonstrating trust and confidence in the team member. The fact that these jobs are important also suggests that they may be used to develop staff.

Session C

Low importance/high urgency   Team leaders may feel that they don't have time to delegate jobs in this category, and that it is quicker to do them themselves. But if team members already have experience in doing these jobs, then the time taken to delegate again will not be great and team leaders can focus on more important work.

Low importance/low urgency   If the job is not important and not urgent, team leaders may question whether the job has to be done at all. However, where jobs still need to be done, they can be effectively delegated to team members.

There are some key advantages in delegating work of lower priority.

- You ensure that these jobs are done.
- You will have time to go through the delegation process thoroughly with jobs that are not urgent. This will be especially necessary when the jobs themselves are important or when you are delegating to an inexperienced team member
- When you delegate jobs that are of medium to low importance, you will have more time to focus on those which you consider are important.

3.4 Routine jobs

As a team leader you will have responsibility for carrying out a range of routine jobs, for example, monitoring and regular reporting. It makes sense to delegate some of these activities to team members, so that they develop the skills and experience to do these jobs themselves. Delegation here helps to increase team member involvement in the overall work of the section, and can foster appreciation of the purpose and importance of routine activities – which can sometimes seem pointless and time-consuming to team members.

3.5 Attractive jobs

Although not all the tasks that are worth delegating appeal to team members it is worth including some which are generally seen as desirable. Such jobs can be used to reward staff for good performance. Here is an example.

> An international company which has a large workforce based in France regularly sends groups of managers to the UK in order to improve their use of English. They are based at a language school in Bath for two weeks at a time and, although it is a working course, it is also viewed by those who come as a very pleasant trip. Each time a group comes over, which is about every three months, a member of the company's training

Session C

department comes with them. Sometimes the head of training comes with the group herself, but often she sends other members of her department instead. Partly this is to improve their own English language, but it is also an example of her willingness to delegate some of the attractive parts of her job.

Activity 19

10 mins

We have looked at some of the kinds of jobs which may be suitable for delegation. Now relate these to your own work. Select two tasks you currently carry out which fit into each of the categories of job listed below. Your tasks can fall into more than one category.

Tasks which team members can do as well as or better than you.

_____
_____

Tasks which serve to develop individuals.

_____
_____

Tasks which are of low to medium priority.

_____
_____

Tasks which are routine.

_____
_____

Tasks which appeal to team members.

_____
_____

Session C

The tasks which you have identified may all be suitable for delegation. However, you may also find that those which are most suitable for delegation fall into more than one category. For example, we would argue that a task which is of medium priority and which will also help to develop staff is a prime candidate for delegation.

4 Delegating to volunteers

As a manager, you may well have a responsibility for developing the skills and experience of volunteers. But you can only delegate to volunteers to the extent that they want to accept. With paid employees, you have the last resort of being able to instruct them to do something, but you don't have this option with volunteers. In fact, you have to keep them positively interested and committed all the time or you will lose them. While paid employees may tell you that they are not happy, volunteers are more likely just to stop coming.

It is therefore critically important to share what are seen to be the attractive and sought after tasks equally and fairly. You need to get to know which tasks volunteers regard as attractive. Some volunteers may be keen to acquire new skills and new experiences which will stand them in good stead for paid work in other areas. But you may also find that a particular youth club activity or a shift that fits in well with school hours represent the coveted jobs.

5 Which of your tasks can you delegate?

A work diary is a useful way of finding out the activities we carry out at work.

Session C

Activity 20
15 mins

Complete your work diary twice a day over at least three fairly typical working days.

Keep the recording system as simple as possible, so that you really do use it. For example, use a log sheet something like the one shown below.

Name			Date	Sheet Number	
Time		Activity	Type of activity (planning, organizing, motivating, controlling, other)	Duration (min.)	Notes or comments
Started	Finished				

EXTENSION 1
Making a record of all your work activities may be time-consuming, but it is often very revealing – not only for planning delegation, but also for time managment. Extension 1 looks at how to use your time wisely.

Many people are surprised when they review their work diaries to discover how they actually spend their time. Many find there is much greater scope for delegation than they first thought.

46

Session C

Activity 21

15 mins

When you have collected the information about how you spend your time, you then need to analyse it.

First of all separate all the activities which you **need to deal with yourself**. These may be tasks that come under the headings of planning or organizing work and motivating and controlling your workteam, or tasks which your organization requires you to do yourself.

Now put the rest of the tasks under the following headings. They may fall under more than one heading.

Team members competent to do	Developmental	Low to medium priority	Routine	Attractive

You should find that most of the tasks under these headings are suitable for delegation. Circle the ones which you now feel you should have delegated.

Session C

Your work in this Activity shows the potential scope for delegating parts of your recent work. You are likely to find that if you had delegated some of your work, you would have had more time to spend on more important tasks.

To decide which of your current tasks you can delegate, you have to work out priorities.

Activity 22

20 mins

S/NVQ C12.1

This Activity is the first in a series of eleven Activities for which your responses may together form the basis of evidence for your S/NVQ portfolio. If you are intending to take this course of action, it might be better to write your answers on separate sheets of paper.

Make a 'To do' list for the next three to five days. Write down all the things you need to do in the space below.

_____
_____
_____
_____
_____
_____
_____
_____
_____
_____
_____

When you have done this, analyse your list.

Write an 'S' besides those which you feel only you can do.

Write a 'D' next to all those that you immediately feel you can delegate.

Session C

EXTENSION 2
Extension 2 deals with the central problem of all managers: how to get the best out of themselves and their workteam.

When you have separated those tasks you plan to do yourself and those you can delegate, you should prioritize your tasks by considering how important and how urgent each one is. This will help you to decide the order in which to tackle them, and also to see which of them you could delegate to others.

The way you prioritize tasks depends on your own experience and judgement of what is important. Only you can assess the consequences of not doing the job on time or to the standard needed.

One way of sorting out your priorities is to place each job in the appropriate place on a chart showing scales of importance and urgency, like the one shown earlier (page 42).

Let's see how this works by looking at a case study.

On Tuesday evening before leaving work, Sandra Wilkinson drew up the following list of tasks which she needed to do the next day. She wrote comments beside each one. The list of tasks was as follows.

Job		Comments
A	Arrange farewell presentation	For Thursday lunchtime
B	Answer memo from the general manager	Task delegated to me by my boss
C	Complete return for the finance department	Already delayed through my having to wait for information
D	Prepare information for computer input	Deadline 5 pm Friday
E	Check suppliers' acceptance of new specification	Should be done before new contract starts
F	Prepare unfair dismissal case for industrial tribunal	Must be suitable for my boss to present by Friday
G	Write up minutes of team meeting	Promised for Thursday
H	Complete report on accident which happened yesterday	Statutory requirement: must complete while fresh in my mind
I	Collect/analyse information about results of quality improvement project	Needed for report to my boss by end of month
J	Prepare briefing to team on new contract	Briefing meeting Thursday

49

Session C

Sandra first identified those tasks which she felt only she could do. These were: B, F, H and J.

Then she rated the tasks according to their importance and urgency in the following chart.

[Chart: A quadrant diagram with axes "High importance" (top), "Low importance" (bottom), "High urgency" (left), "Low urgency" (right). Tasks are plotted as follows: F, H, J in the high urgency/high importance quadrant (upper left); B, D, I in the low urgency/high importance quadrant (upper right); A, G, C in the high urgency/low importance quadrant (lower left); E in the low urgency/low importance quadrant (lower right).]

With this information, Sandra decided that in order to get the tasks done she needed to delegate some of her work.

She decided to delegate parts of task A, although she would have to plan what to say. She also felt tasks D, E and I would be developmental tasks which various members of her team would benefit from doing. She decided to ask an experienced team member to write up the team meeting minutes (Task G) – he had done the job once before. Finally she thought that it would not take her long to complete the return for finance, and she thought that although urgent, she could delay the job until Thursday, if necessary. Of the tasks which she had to do herself, she felt she could delay task B, but the others had to be done on Wednesday.

Activity 23

30 mins

S/NVQ C12.1

This Activity is the second in a series of eleven Activities for which your responses may together form the basis of evidence for your S/NVQ portfolio. If you are intending to take this course of action, it might be better to write your answers on separate sheets of paper.

Session C

This Activity asks you to use the importance/urgency matrix to put your tasks in order of priority.

Make a list of the tasks which you labelled 'D' in Activity 22 and give each one a letter starting from A. We've given you space for up to ten tasks, but you can add more if you choose.

A _____

B _____

C _____

D _____

E _____

F _____

G _____

H _____

I _____

J _____

Now prioritize them by placing them in appropriate positions in the chart below.

High importance

High urgency ⊢————————————⊣ Low urgency

Low importance

Session C

This prioritizing of tasks should show you tasks which you need to carry out yourself and which ones may be suitable for delegating. Now consider which of these tasks:

■ staff are competent to do;
_____
_____
_____

■ are developmental;
_____
_____

■ are routine;
_____
_____
_____

■ are attractive to do.
_____
_____
_____

I hope you have seen that prioritizing your work according to importance and urgency helps you to see where you need to direct your efforts and your opportunities for delegating.

Activity 24 · 10 mins

S/NVQ C12.1

This Activity is the third in a series of eleven Activities for which your responses may together form the basis of evidence for your S/NVQ portfolio. If you are intending to take this course of action, it might be better to write your answers on separate sheets of paper.

Select a job which you want to delegate to a team member. It may be one of those which you identified in Activity 22 or Activity 23.

Session C

As you work through the rest of the workbook you will go through the process of planning and controlling the delegation. So you should choose a job that is reasonably challenging and interesting.

Briefly describe the job here.

_____
_____
_____

Now describe the benefits of delegating this job:

- to you as team leader;

_____
_____
_____
_____

- to the person who will be carrying out the delegated task;

_____
_____
_____
_____

- to the organization.

_____
_____
_____
_____

6 Selecting a team member for delegation

All of your team members can benefit from delegation, and you should look for opportunities to delegate to everyone in your team. But if you have a particular job to delegate, you need to think about who is the 'right' person to do the job.

Session C

This involves considering the requirements of the job and the needs of your team members. Let's look at the requirements of the job first.

There are four questions to ask.

- What experience, expertise, skills and attitudes are needed to do the job? The job may require a high level of technical know-how or previous experience, which only certain members of your team possess.
- How urgent is the job? If you need the job done urgently, you will have less time to spend briefing and supporting an inexperienced team member. You may want to delegate an urgent job to someone who has done a similar task before, and who is already competent to do it.
- What are the consequences of missing deadlines, or making mistakes? By thinking about the importance of getting the job right first time and the deadline for completing it, you can judge the level of risk you are prepared to take in giving the task to someone who has never done it before.
- What is the most economical way of getting the job done?

Let's look at an example to explain this last point.

Activity 25 · 5 mins

Bill Pearce, a team leader of a graphics design shop, was complaining to his boss that he found himself spending a large part of his working day using the photocopying machine.

If you were Bill's manager, how would you recommend Bill overcomes the problem?

_____
_____
_____
_____

You may agree that managers who spend much of their time photocopying materials are not using their time cost effectively. Surely the task could more often be given to somebody whose time represents a lower cost to the organization? The activity shows how particular jobs are often done at a totally uneconomic rate.

Session C

Sometimes you may decide it is worth using more resources in delegating a job than absolutely necessary, especially if you plan to use delegation for team development.

This takes us on to thinking about who among the team members is the best person to carry out the job.

We have seen that you may want to delegate tasks to team members who are already competent to carry them out. In this way you are acknowledging and making use of the expertise and skills of team members. However, it is not always appropriate to select the person whose skills and experience are the most suitable for the job.

Delegation is an important technique for developing competence across your team. As a manager you need to be thinking about developing your team members so that they are able to meet the current challenges of their work, and are prepared to meet future challenges. So it may be a good idea to delegate a particular job to someone who needs to learn how to do it as part of a development programme, or to gain further experience in carrying out a task of which he or she already has limited knowledge.

Again there are a number of questions to ask.

- Who will find the job challenging and/or interesting?
- Who will benefit from taking on the job?
- Who has the skills, expertise and attitudes needed to do the job?
- Who has carried out a similar job before?
- Who do you think has the necessary skills, but has not yet used them for a job like this?
- Who could do the job with some coaching or help from another member of the team?
- Who is available to do the job?
- Can you reorganize someone's work so that he or she becomes available to take on the job?
- Is there someone who would regard doing the job as a form of recognition and/or reward?

> Bear in mind that delegation can be used as part of training and development.

Session C

Activity 26

30 mins

S/NVQ C12.1

This Activity is the fourth in a series of eleven Activities for which your responses may together form the basis of evidence for your S/NVQ portfolio. If you are intending to take this course of action, it might be better to write your answers on separate sheets of paper.

This Activity helps you to work out the best person to take on the job you have chosen to delegate.

First consider the requirements of the job, and write notes under the headings below.

Skills, expertise and attitudes required.

_____
_____
_____
_____

How urgent the job is.

_____
_____
_____
_____

Consequences of not getting it right.

_____
_____
_____
_____

Most cost-effective way of doing the job.

_____
_____
_____
_____

Session C

Now think about your team members by answering the following questions.

Who will find the job challenging and/or interesting?
_____
_____

Who will benefit from taking on the job?
_____
_____

Who has the skills, expertise and attitudes needed to do the job?
_____
_____

Who has carried out a similar job before?
_____
_____

Who has the necessary skills, but has not yet used them for a job like this?
_____
_____

Who could do the job with some coaching or help from another member of the team?
_____
_____

Who is available to do the job?
_____
_____

Can you reorganize someone's work so that he or she becomes available to take on the job?
_____
_____

Session C

Is this job suitable as a form of reward or recognition? If so, to whom might it be delegated for this purpose?

_____

_____

In the light of your comments about the job itself and your team members, who is the best person to do the job?

_____

_____

I hope you agree that the systematic approach taken in this activity helps you to take account of all the angles when selecting the most suitable person to carry out a delegated task.

You may find it useful to adopt a similar approach when you are preparing to delegate other tasks.

EXTENSION 3
Extension 3 looks at how to delegate tasks to your team, rather than simply to individuals.

By now you should have chosen a suitable task for delegating and selected the most appropriate person to do the job. You have gone through the stages of preparing for delegation. In the next session you will be carrying out the delegation.

Self-assessment 3

20 mins

Here is a list of tasks which a manager has drawn up.

a See Carole about being late in to work. ☐
b Deal with staff grievance. ☐
c Investigate the problem with no. 2 machine – used by operators. ☐
d Write up minutes of team meeting. ☐
e Organize date, place and time for quality improvement project meeting. ☐
f Brief supplier on new product specification. ☐
g Prepare month's production figures for manager. ☐
h Liaise with training about team's health and safety needs. ☐

1 Tick those which you think may be suitable for delegating.

Session C

2 Which ones are definitely unsuitable for delegating and why?

3 Why might you delegate a task to a team member who has not had experience in doing the task?

4 Why might you delegate a task to a team member who has the expertise and experience in doing the task?

Answers to these questions can be found on page 96.

Session C

7 Summary

- You cannot delegate all your work. Examples of **work you cannot delegate** include:
  - work of a confidential nature;
  - activities your organization requires you to carry out yourself;
  - work which you do not have the authority to delegate.

- Jobs which you **can delegate** to others include those:
  - which can be done just as well by a member of your workteam;
  - for which a member of your workteam is technically more able, or has easier access to the relevant information;
  - which help to develop team members and which may be interesting and/or challenging;
  - of medium or low priority;
  - which are routine;
  - which are attractive, and may be part of your system of recognition and reward to team members.

- If you **manage volunteers**, you must keep them committed and motivated to do the work. This may mean offering them new experiences and opportunities to develop new skills, but it may also mean getting to know the coveted jobs and allocating them fairly and equally.

- To find the right person to do a job, you need to consider first the **requirements of the job**, and then the **needs of your team members**.

- In considering the requirements of the job, think about the following.
  - The skills and expertise needed to do the job.
  - The importance and urgency of the job.
  - The degree of risk you are able to take.
  - The most cost-effective way of doing the job.

- The right person for the job may be:
  - the person with the necessary skills, expertise and experience;
  - someone who has the skills and expertise, but has not yet had experience in doing the job;
  - someone whose skills you want to develop through delegating;
  - someone who has the time to do the work, or whose workload can be reorganized so they are available to do it;
  - a person whose work and commitment you would like to recognize and/or reward in a practical way.

Session D
Carrying out delegation

1 Introduction

You have begun the process of delegating effectively by selecting an appropriate job to delegate and by choosing a member of your workteam to carry it out. In this session you will continue the process by carrying out the delegation. This involves:

- setting clear objectives;
- planning the delegated task;
- monitoring the task when it is being carried out;
- reviewing the results of the delegation with the team member.

You may recall that we introduced the full process in Session A.

Session D

2 Setting objectives

To be effective everyone in an organization needs to know their particular objectives – so they know where they are heading. Clear objectives allow everyone to:

- know precisely what has to be done;
- judge when it has been achieved.

So when you are delegating you need to write down objectives that the person who is carrying out the task can understand and use.

An effective objective is SMART. This stands for the following.

- **Specific** – stating exactly what has to be achieved, although not **how** the job should be done.
- **Measurable** – so that you can tell when the task has been done properly; it might involve a description of the results of the task, or standards for doing the job.
- **Achievable** – the objective has to be realistic in the circumstances, given the resources that are available, for example, people, equipment, materials, money, information and time, and the people who will carry it out must agree to it.
- **Relevant** – the objective must be seen as relating both to the job roles of those who are to achieve the objective and to the wider objectives of the organization.
- **Time bound** – it is important to give some guidance about deadlines and time-frames for achieving the objective, again, these should be realistic.

It should also contribute to the objectives of the team or section.

So in order to write SMART objectives you need to know exactly what it is you want done, what resources will be needed to do the job and when it is to be done.

Session D

Activity 27

15 mins

Imagine you have been given the following set of objectives.

'The job involves finding out about customer complaints in this section.

At the end of this task you will have:

- collected information about customer complaints between April last year and end March this year – using data stored in the customer complaints file in Jackie's office area;
- organized and summarized that information;
- presented findings to the supervisor in a short (3–4 page) report in hard copy and in Word, using tables or charts to summarize the information.'

How SMART are these objectives? What additional information, if any, is needed to make the objectives SMART? Write your ideas below under the following headings.

Specific.

_____
_____
_____

Measurable.

_____
_____
_____

Achievable.

_____
_____
_____

Relevant.

_____
_____
_____

Session D

Time bound.

You probably agree that the objectives do not meet the SMART criteria. Although we know the period to be investigated, the objectives do not specify which customer complaints should be examined and they do not state what sort of information is needed. There are no details about how to organize the information, for example, does it need to be organized by type of customer, type of complaint or response to the complaint? We have more details about handing the information to the supervisor, but there is no time guideline, so we don't know when the job has to be completed. There is some indication of resources in the mention of the customer complaints file, and we will need to make sure we will have access to Word on computer in order to write the report. The vague wording of the objectives will make it difficult to know when they have been achieved, although the presentation of the report is one indication.

Before we could agree to these objectives, some important details will have to be sorted out.

To make the objectives SMART they could be refined as follows.

'Senior management have asked for a report about how well the customer care policy is working. To do this we need to find out how we have handled all customer complaints over the past year.

Your job is to:

- collect information about all customer complaints between April last year and end March this year – using data stored in the customer complaints file held in Jackie's office area;
- organize and summarize that information under the following headings:

- type of customer;
- nature of the complaint;
- how the complaint was made;
- who handled the complaint;
- how the complaint was dealt with;
- response times;

- present findings to the supervisor in a short (3–4 page) report in hard copy and on disk in the normal program (Word), using tables or charts to summarize the information.

The deadline for this job is 15 May.'

64

Session D

Notice that the objectives here include a brief statement about why it is necessary. While it could be argued that the purpose of a job is not strictly part of the objectives, it certainly helps people if they understand why they are going to do it. Look at the following case.

> Rebecca Davis was about to rush off to a meeting with clients, but she had time for a quick word with Steve Gould first. 'Look, I have to go, but I've just heard from the warehouse that the printers have finally delivered the brochures. Can you arrange to have them transferred over here by 2.30 pm at the latest?' Steve agreed and Rebecca disappeared out of the room. Steve arranged for the warehouse to interrupt another job and deliver the 10,000 brochures to reception by 2.00 pm. At 2.40 pm Rebecca came out of her meeting and found Steve. 'Where are the brochures?' Steve explained that they were all down in reception. Rebecca pulled a face. 'But I only need two or three of them to show to the clients.'

Just a simple misunderstanding, perhaps. But if Rebecca had explained **why** she needed the brochures, then she would have saved herself some embarrassment, and she would have saved Steve and the warehouse some valuable time.

Activity 28

20 mins

S/NVQ C12.1

This Activity is the fifth in a series of eleven Activities for which your responses may together form the basis of evidence for your S/NVQ portfolio. If you are intending to take this course of action, it might be better to write your answers on separate sheets of paper.

Think about what is involved in carrying out the task you are planning to delegate. Think about what the team member who will be doing the work will require to complete the task successfully.

When you have considered these aspects, write SMART objectives for the task you are planning to delegate. Make sure that these objectives link up with the wider objectives of your team or section.

Session D

_____
_____
_____
_____
_____
_____
_____
_____

Check whether your objectives are linked to the work of your team and that they are:

- specific – so that the task is clearly defined and explained;
- measurable – so that the team member can tell when he or she has successfully achieved the task;
- achievable – the resources required are available;
- relevant – everyone involved is clear why they're being asked to do the task;
- time bound – there is a clear deadline for completion of the task.

Be prepared to improve your objectives. You may find it helpful to put yourself in the shoes of the person to whom you will be delegating. Will the team member understand exactly what is required in doing the job when he or she reads them?

3 Planning

When you have set the objectives you need to give further consideration to the task you are delegating and then discuss it with the team member. In this section we look at:

- planning resources;
- briefing the team member.

Session D

3.1 Planning resources

When you are delegating you need to give the team member the necessary authority and resources to carry out the task.

Consider how you will make sure that the team member has the necessary authority to carry out the task, particularly where this involves other people. You may have to inform others that the team member will be acting on your behalf. Other people are just one of the resources that may be required to do the job. How will you make sure that the resources needed are available? For example, do you need to give the team member a budget to work with?

Activity 29

15 mins

Portfolio of evidence — S/NVQ C12.1

This Activity is the sixth in a series of eleven Activities for which your responses may together form the basis of evidence for your S/NVQ portfolio. If you are intending to take this course of action, it might be better to write your answers on separate sheets of paper.

In Activity 28 you developed objectives for the task you are planning to delegate.

Now consider the resources you need to allocate to your team member. Make a note of these resources in the left-hand column. In the right-hand column write any action you need to take to make sure these resources are available.

Resources needed	How to make them available

Session D

You may have considered the following resources:

- people;
- machinery and equipment;
- materials;
- finance;
- information;
- time.

As we have seen, you keep overall responsibility for the task you are delegating, so it is up to you to make sure the task is completed successfully and all the objectives are achieved. Plan to monitor the important parts of the job while it is underway. You may want to monitor the use of resources, as well as the way the job is done.

You should also plan to review it when it is completed. Consider suitable rewards for work that is done well. These can be of many different forms, such as praise, greater work independence, or maybe something tangible, such as a bonus or promotion.

We will look at monitoring and reviewing in more detail later in this session, but you do have to think about these aspects while you are planning.

3.2 Briefing the team member

EXTENSION 1
Extension 1 looks at effective communications and at making the most of meetings.

Briefing the team member about the task is an opportunity to refine the plan and amend it where necessary.

Bear in mind that you are not simply informing a team member about the task. You want to give this person responsibility to do the job so you want to gain their interest, involvement and commitment. The aim of the discussion is to reach agreement on all aspects of the task.

The best way of doing this is to ask them for their views, and to be prepared to modify your ideas in the light of their contribution. Use the briefing as an opportunity to develop the plan with the team member. Remember that the team member is going to carry out the work, so they need to be comfortable with it.

> Look on the briefing as an opportunity to **consult** rather than simply to **inform**.

Here is a suggested approach to briefing.

- Explain the task and what you want to achieve. You may want to explain that you see it as a development opportunity for the team member, or that you are delegating the job to the team member because you know they have the skills, experience and expertise to do a good job.

Session D

- Ask the team member to tell you how they would do the job, rather than instructing them how to do it. In this way you will get a clear idea about the team member's approach and can judge whether your plan for controlling the job is pitched at the right level.
- Ask the team member to decide what resources they think they will need to meet the objectives for the job, including any help they will need from you. Then discuss your views on resources and how you will make them available.
- Ask the team member to estimate the time it is likely to take. Then discuss with them your views on the timing, interim deadlines and so on.
- Agree how you will keep track of progress and offer support and guidance, so that the team member can come to you to discuss any ideas or problems they have.

It is important to give the team member enough time to reflect and consider how they will do the job. Bear in mind that although you are familiar with the task, it is all new to the team member. You may need to schedule a follow-up meeting so the team member can come back to you with their thoughts and suggestions on how they will carry out the job.

Activity 30

30 mins

Portfolio of evidence

S/NVQs C12.1, C12.2

This Activity is the seventh in a series of eleven Activities for which your responses may together form the basis of evidence for your S/NVQ portfolio. If you are intending to take this course of action, it might be better to write your answers on separate sheets of paper.

Write out a checklist or briefing document for delegating on which both you and the team member can record the agreed details of the task. The document should cover all the areas you need to consider when discussing the task with the team member.

Check that your document includes headings and space for the following information.

- The purpose of the task.
- The objectives.
- The resources available.
- The support available.
- How to monitor the task and keep track of progress.
- When and how you will review the task.

Session D

Activity 31

20 mins

S/NVQs C12.1, C12.2

This Activity is the eighth in a series of eleven Activities for which your responses may together form the basis of evidence for your S/NVQ portfolio. If you are intending to take this course of action, it might be better to write your answers on separate sheets of paper.

Use your checklist to brief your team member on the task you have chosen to delegate.

Now make brief notes on how well the briefing went by answering the following questions.

How well did you describe the background and purpose of the job?

_____
_____
_____

How did you explain why you have selected the team member to do the job?

_____
_____
_____

How well did you talk through with the team member:

- the objectives?

  _____

- the resource requirements?

  _____

- how you and others can provide support?

  _____

- how to monitor progress?

  _____

- how to review the task?

  _____

Session D

What contributions did the team member make to the discussion?
___
___
___
___
___

How would you describe the team member's attitude towards the task? (Committed, enthusiastic, confident, apprehensive?)
___
___
___
___

How successful was the briefing?
___
___
___

What will you do next time to improve the briefing?
___
___
___

A successful briefing depends on good planning and effective communication on the part of the manager. This means listening carefully, responding appropriately and checking understanding. Remember that a successful briefing will lead to agreement about the task. You will feel confident that the job you have delegated is in good hands, and that the team member knows what to do, how to do it, by when and with what results. You will also feel that the team member is committed to doing the job well.

After the briefing the team member should begin to carry out the job. Although you have handed over the job you will still need to check on progress through monitoring.

Session D

4 Monitoring the delegated task

By monitoring a job, you stay in control, you will be able to see potential problems at an early stage and you can guide your team member to make any necessary changes to keep the job on course.

Remember that the level of direct control you have over a job is related to the amount of trust you have in the team member doing a good job. Bear in mind how the team member is likely to respond if you show little confidence in their abilities and keep intervening in the job. Whenever you delegate, you are taking some risk, because you are sharing your responsibility for the job with another person.

The key to monitoring work that you delegate is to agree the following with the team member at the start.

- Objectives – what you want to achieve.
- Time scales and deadlines – what aspects of the job need to be completed by when.
- Critical activities – the key parts of a job, on which the success of the whole job depends.

You can then agree to monitor the job against these benchmarks. There are many ways of monitoring, as shown below.

- Having informal discussions with a team member when you meet him or her on-the-job.
- Collecting information, such as operating temperatures of machinery, attendance records, numbers of telephone calls made, number of client contacts made.
- Arranging to review progress with the team member perhaps by a report or an informal meeting. Progress reviews may be planned in advance and determined by time, stages in the job or other factors.
- Agreeing with a team member that they will come to you if they predict any problems or difficulties in getting the job done as previously agreed.
- Examining the results of work – a manufactured product, a report, etc.
- Observing a team member carrying out some aspect of the job, a discussion with a customer or colleague, for example.

Team members are usually actively involved in collecting, recording and communicating information for monitoring. Although this information may

Session D

come to you so that you can keep overall control of the work, team members themselves often know when the work is going well and when a job is going off-course. They can usually suggest solutions, if encouraged to do so.

By getting team members to monitor aspects of a task themselves, you are giving them scope to control the work, to take appropriate action if they foresee any problems. This shows that you trust them.

If you uncover a potential problem while monitoring the delegated task, be tactful in pointing it out to the team member, for example, choose a quiet place where you won't be overheard. Encourage the team member to offer solutions. Bear in mind that your aim is to support the team member and help him or her be successful.

Activity 32

15 mins

S/NVQ C12.2

This Activity is the ninth in a series of eleven Activities for which your responses may together form the basis of evidence for your S/NVQ portfolio. If you are intending to take this course of action, it might be better to write your answers on separate sheets of paper.

What methods are you using to monitor the job you have delegated?

_____
_____
_____

How involved is the team member in monitoring?

_____
_____
_____

Think about the level of direct control you have over the task, and the level of trust this shows that you have in your team member.

Mark the spectrum below to indicate your level of control and trust.

high control   low control

low trust   high trust

73

Session D

It is worth thinking about whether you have chosen an appropriate level of control and trust. You can do this when you come to review the delegated task.

5 Reviewing the delegation

Although you may review progress while the job is underway, you will want to carry out a thorough review soon after a delegated task has been completed. It is an important opportunity for you and your team member to consider the success – or otherwise – of the task, to learn from the experience and plan improvements for the future.

Your review may cover different aspects of the task, including the process of delegating. For example, you may want to look at:

- the extent to which the objectives have been met or have had to be changed;
- the use made of resources;
- the effectiveness of support given to the team member;
- how well the task was monitored and controlled;
- any difficulties or problems;
- the team member's performance in carrying out the job and how he or she can build on what has been learned.

When reviewing a delegated task, it is best to let your team member get the praise for work successfully done, but to accept the blame yourself when things have gone wrong. The reason for this is that you have to accept overall responsibility, including the decision to delegate in the first place.

An important part of any review will be the feedback that you give to the team member on their performance.

Session D

Activity 33

5 mins

Note down what you think is the purpose of giving feedback to a team member about their performance in carrying out a delegated task.

_____
_____
_____
_____

I hope you agree that the aim of giving feedback is to help the team member learn from the experience – both the successes and failures – so that they can do better next time. It is the key to encouraging staff to develop, so it is an important part of your responsibilities as a manager.

Feedback should be designed to improve performance.

As a team leader you will probably give informal feedback to team members frequently, but it is also important to set aside some time to have a one-to-one meeting with the team member to give formal feedback.

Giving feedback on good performance does not usually represent a problem – as long as you **still** do give feedback. Successful people need as much development as unsuccessful ones. Feedback on good performance should encourage team members to reflect, identify what has contributed to their success, and consider what they would do differently next time.

When we have to point out mistakes and poor performance we have to work hard to avoid criticizing. Think about how you react when someone criticizes you. Most people agree that if they feel they are being criticized, they get upset or resentful, make excuses or stop listening.

If feedback makes someone feel bad or useless, then it has not served its purpose. Even if you have to point out mistakes, it is important that what you say is encouraging and designed to increase motivation.

Here are eight simple guidelines for giving effective feedback.

1 **Never give feedback when you are angry or frustrated.** You need to be calm, thinking about solving any problem and moving forward.

Session D

2 **Give praise where it is due.** It is all too easy to forget the aspects of a job that have been done well, especially when there are other problems. Be specific in your praise, highlighting those aspects of a job that were handled well, or where the team member showed good judgement.

3 **Encourage the person to whom you are giving feedback to contribute their ideas.** These might include what they think they did well, what went wrong and why, and how they would do things next time. By getting the person to assess their own performance you will have a clear idea of areas of agreement, and areas where you need to give more guidance about mistakes.

4 **Be specific about mistakes.** Give exact instances so that the other person can recognize where mistakes were made.

5 **Criticize the action or the behaviour, not the person.** For example, don't say, 'You were wrong to . . .', instead say that a particular action was wrong.

6 **Investigate the cause of any difficulty.** Was it an instance of bad judgement, was it to do with lack of resources, was it owing to lack of support from you?

7 **Offer support.** How can you help the person solve the problem for the future? Does the person need training? Do they need more support from you or from a team member?

8 **End on a positive note by looking forward to making improvements next time around.** Looking ahead enables both you and the person to whom you are giving feedback to put any mistakes of the past to rest, and move forward.

This kind of feedback is an important aspect of your responsibilities for the development of staff. It doesn't cost anything, except your time, but it's this kind of attention which can make a real difference to people's careers and commitment.

Activity 34

30 mins

S/NVQs C12.2, C12.3

This Activity is the tenth in a series of eleven Activities for which your responses may together form the basis of evidence for your S/NVQ portfolio. If you are intending to take this course of action, it might be better to write your answers on separate sheets of paper.

Session D

Plan a feedback session with your team member to review his or her performance in carrying out the delegated task.

When is the review session?
_____

What did the team member do well?
_____
_____
_____
_____

What mistakes were made?
_____
_____
_____
_____

Why do **you** think mistakes were made?
_____
_____
_____
_____

What suggestions do you have for making improvements in the future?
_____
_____
_____
_____

What are the next steps for the team member, for instance, more responsibility and involvement in the team, some coaching, a training course?
_____
_____
_____
_____

Session D

You may ask the team member to plan for the session in a similar way, by considering what went well, where improvements could be made next time and so on. Your team member's self-assessment is important, and you could use it as evidence in your portfolio.

Use your plan to carry out the feedback session. Then assess how well it went in the next activity.

Activity 35
20 mins

S/NVQs C12.2, C12.3

This Activity is the last in a series of eleven Activities for which your responses may together form the basis of evidence for your S/NVQ portfolio. If you are intending to take this course of action, it might be better to write your answers on separate sheets of paper.

Assess your feedback session by answering the following questions.

What aspects of the feedback session went well? Why?

_____
_____
_____
_____

What aspects of the session could have gone better? Why?

_____
_____
_____
_____

What contribution did the team member make to the session?

_____
_____
_____
_____

Session D

How did the team member feel about the feedback you gave? For example, were you able to agree about his or her performance? Did you agree on the next steps?

_____
_____
_____
_____

What will you do differently the next time you give feedback?

_____
_____
_____
_____

Giving constructive feedback is not easy, and it takes practice to give feedback which helps team members improve performance. If you have identified areas for improvement, you are working towards developing your feedback skills.

To delegate effectively you need to use a range of management skills: planning, organizing, communicating, briefing, supporting, controlling and giving feedback.

Delegating will give you more time to concentrate on your important work, but, more significantly perhaps, by using the process of delegating and delegating effectively, you will also develop your team and your relationship of trust with team members.

Session D

Self-assessment 4

1 Describe the features of a SMART objective.

S _____

M _____

A _____

R _____

T _____

For questions 2 to 5, complete the sentences with a suitable word or words.

2 When briefing a team member make sure that you and they _____ all aspects of the task.

3 _____ involves collecting information about how well a task is going, and enables you or the team member to take action to prevent problems from becoming serious.

4 After the delegated task has been done, you should _____ its successes and failures, so that you can make improvements next time.

5 Part of a review involves giving _____ to the team member on his or her performance.

6 Complete the eight guidelines for giving constructive feedback listed below.

a Never give feedback when you are _____.

b Give _____ where it is due.

c Encourage the person to whom you are giving feedback to _____.

d Be specific about _____.

e Criticise the _____, not the person.

f Investigate the _____ of any difficulty.

g Offer _____.

h End on _____.

Answers to these questions can be found on page 97.

Session D

6 Summary

- **Objectives** state what you want to achieve.

- Objectives should be **SMART**.
  - Specific.
  - Measurable.
  - Achievable.
  - Relevant.
  - Time bound.

- When planning the delegation, make sure that:
  - the necessary **authority** for carrying out the task is given;
  - the necessary **resources** are made available.

- The purpose of **briefing** a team member when delegating to them is to reach agreement about all aspects of the task, including the objectives and to gain their **commitment** to do the task.

- When discussing the task **ask the team member** how they would do it, what resources they think they would need, and so on, and then discuss your views.

- **Monitoring** enables you to keep track of progress and take action to keep a job on course if there are problems.

- You can use formal and informal methods to monitor a delegated task and encourage team members to take part in monitoring.

- Make sure you are available to offer **support** to the team member when needed.

- Your **review** of the delegation when the task is completed should include giving **feedback** on the team member's performance.

- Giving feedback is an important part of your responsibility to develop staff.

- Give feedback sensitively in order to help the team member improve his or her performance in the future.

Performance checks

1 Quick quiz

Question 1 What does delegation mean?

Question 2 Briefly explain how delegation can improve decision-making.

Question 3 How do you keep overall responsibility for a job which you have delegated?

Question 4 Describe the stages in the process of effective delegation.

Performance checks

Question 5 How can you use delegation to develop trust in your team?

Question 6 What is over-delegation?

Question 7 Give one key advantage to you – as a team leader – of delegating.

Question 8 What improvements in team or individual performance are likely to result from effective delegation?

Question 9 Which tasks ought you to delegate?

Question 10 Can you delegate your responsibility for health and safety?

Question 11 Why do you need to set objectives for a task you are delegating?

Question 12 What resources might need to be allocated to a team member when you are delegating?

Performance checks

Question 13   What are you seeking to achieve when briefing a team member about a delegated task?

_____
_____
_____

Question 14   Why do you need to monitor a delegated task?

_____
_____
_____

Question 15   What is the aim of giving feedback?

_____
_____

Answers to these questions can be found on pages 98–99.

2 Workbook assessment

60 mins

Read the following case study and then answer the questions which follow, writing your answers on a separate sheet of paper.

Charlie Scrimshaw is the head of the contracts department of a large advertising agency. He started work with the company originally as a member of the sales team, and is much happier when talking to people rather than sitting behind a desk. As a result of this preference, his paperwork is seldom up to date.

The business is passing through a period of rapid expansion and, as a result of this, a number of new members have been added to Charlie's team, bringing the total for whom he is responsible to thirty-five. Unfortunately, as control systems are not something with which Charlie is familiar, he has tended to try to get along without them. One result of this is that he doesn't plan very far ahead. He says he

Performance checks

cannot find time for planning, as he has too much to do which is concerned with current work. Other members of his department have been heard to describe his management approach as 'lurching from one immediate crisis to the next'.

Charlie believes in what he refers to as an 'open door' policy of managing, making himself always available to members of his workteam whenever they go to his office. He regards this as an important part of his team building, but unfortunately it results in his being constantly interrupted, often for rather trivial reasons. Charlie does not believe in spending a lot of time over making decisions; rather, he regards himself as a 'man of action'. Sometimes, however, his first decision proves to be not very suitable and so after consulting with others, he often quickly changes his mind. A few of Charlie's team members were discussing his method of making decisions during their coffee break the other day. One of them described him as coming to conclusions 'with his mind uncluttered with facts', whilst another said that getting decisions from him was rather like making an instant cup of coffee, 'just add water and stir'.

As a group, they generally agreed that he was a nice guy and a good salesman, but they were concerned that he seemed to spend little time making sure that targets were likely to be met, and only took notice when things had already gone badly astray.

1. What do you think ought to be done at a higher level in the company in order to assist Charlie generally with his supervisory problems?

2. Suggest how Charlie could find the time in which to carry out some forward planning.

3. What can Charlie do to change from his crisis management to being more in control of things?

4. How could Charlie prevent himself being interrupted by his team unnecessarily, but still maintain a good working relationship with them?

5. If you were Charlie, what would you do to make sure you were aware of approaching target dates in time to take any necessary corrective action?

Your complete answer to this assessment need not be longer than a single page.

Performance checks

3 Work-based assignment

S/NVQs C12.1, C12.2, C12.3

The time guide for this assignment gives you an approximate idea of how long it is likely to take you to write up your findings. You will need to spend some additional time gathering information, perhaps talking to colleagues and thinking about the assignment and planning.

Your work on this assignment can form part of your evidence for your S/NVQ portfolio.

For this assignment, you are asked to plan a task which you want to delegate in the light of what you have learned in this workbook. There are three stages to this assignment.

1. Identify which of your jobs in the near future you can delegate.

    - List the jobs you will need to do over the next few days to a week.
    - Put a 'D' beside those which you can delegate.
    - For the rest, put them in an order of priority, using the importance/urgency matrix, and identify those which could be done by other members of your team.
    - Now choose one of your 'to be delegated' tasks to plan for this assignment. Write brief notes to explain why you have chosen this task.

2. Select an appropriate member of your team to carry out the task. Consider the needs of the task and the needs of your team members. You may find it useful to complete a form like the one in Activity 26. Explain the thinking behind your decision.

3. When you have selected the right person to do the job, you should begin to plan it – the third stage.

    Explain how you intend to conduct the briefing. Then draw up notes to help you to explain the task to the team member. The notes should include:

    - suitable objectives for the task;
    - what resources you feel will be needed and how they are to be made available;
    - how the team member can get support and help in doing the task;
    - how the task will be monitored – your role and the role of the team member;

Performance checks

- when and how the task will be reviewed, and what aspects of the task will be reviewed.

You could use the briefing document you drew up in Activity 30 to help you plan the briefing.

Your completed assignment should contain:

- lists and charts showing your jobs, and how you prioritized them, together with an explanation of the 'to be delegated' job which you have selected to plan for this assignment;
- a systematic explanation of why you have selected a particular person from your team to carry out the delegation: you could use the questions in Activity 26 to make sure you explore all the issues;
- a briefing document and a paragraph or two explaining your intended approach to the briefing.

In all, this assignment does not have to be more than three or four pages long.

You can also take your work on this assignment further, by collecting evidence as the delegated task is carried out. For example, you could review how well the briefing session went, show how the task is monitored and how you and the team member reviewed the task. Bear in mind that the team member who carries out the delegation can contribute appropriate evidence, such as an assessment of how he or she fared.

Reflect and review

1 Reflect and review

Now that you have completed your work on *Delegating Effectively*, let us review the workbook objectives. The first objective is:

- you should be better able to explain why delegation is an important management technique.

In the first session we looked at the meaning of delegation and defined some of the terms we would be using. We explored the importance of delegating, and the advantages to you as a team leader of delegating work.

- Have you identified some ways in which delegation can help you, your team members and your organization?

- Have you thought of discussing with your manager and your workteam how you could delegate more effectively to everyone's benefit?

The next objective is

- you should be better able to achieve a balance in the extent to which you delegate.

In Session B we looked at the reasons why people may under-delegate or over-delegate their work.

- Have you decided whether you have got the balance right?

- Do you think that in the past you have tended to under-delegate or over-delegate?

- Have you worked out why?

- Do you see a way of changing the situation?

Reflect and review

Now to the next objective.

- You should be better able to use the process of delegation to delegate effectively.

In Session A we gave an overview of the process of delegating effectively. The first part of the process was about preparing by:

- selecting an appropriate task, and
- choosing the right person to carry out the task.

The second part of the process is to carry out the delegation by:

- setting objectives;
- planning;
- implementing;
- monitoring;
- reviewing.

By going through this process you will be more able to retain control of the delegated task and make the most of the benefits of delegation. In Sessions C and D we took you through the delegation process in some detail, and enabled you to put delegation into practice in your workplace.

- Consider the example of delegation that you prepared for and carried out as part of your work in this workbook.

- How far has the systematic process of delegation helped you develop your skills as an effective delegator?

- What improvements have you noticed in the way you now delegate? Would your workteam agree with this self-assessment?

If you feel that the process of delegation will help you to manage effectively, then you have achieved the following objective.

- You should be able to control your workteam more efficiently.

Although some people fear that delegation means that you have to give up control, we've seen that effective delegation – through the process we have described – can actually help you to control your team more efficiently.

- How do you feel delegation will help you control your workteam?

If you understand how delegation can help to keep you in control of your team, then you have achieved this final objective.

Reflect and review

2 Action plan

Use this plan to further develop for yourself a course of action you want to take. Make a note in the left-hand column of the issues or problems you want to tackle, and then decide what you intend to do, and make a note in column 2.

The resources you need might include time, materials, information or money. You may need to negotiate for some of them, but they could be something easily acquired, like half an hour of somebody's time, or a chapter of a book. Put whatever you need in column 3. No plan means anything without a timescale, so put a realistic target completion date in column 4.

Finally, describe the outcome you want to achieve as a result of this plan, whether it is for your own benefit or advancement, or a more efficient way of doing things.

Desired outcomes				
	1 Issues	2 Action	3 Resources	4 Target completion
Actual outcomes				

Reflect and review

3 Extensions

Extension 1

Book	*Management*
Author	Roger Oldcorn
Edition	Third edition, 1996
Publisher	Pan Books (Business Masters Series), an imprint of Macmillan General Books

Book	*Essential Managers: How to Delegate*
Author	Robert Heller
Edition	1998
Publisher	Dorling Kindersley Essential Managers series

Extension 2

Video	*The Unorganised Manager*, Parts 1, 2 and 3
Produced	1983
Publisher	Video Arts Ltd

The first two parts of *The Unorganised Manager* series show that no matter how efficient managers may think they are, they cannot be fully effective until they learn how to manage their time.

In **Part 1: Damnation** a hard-working manager is so disorganized that he unwittingly makes the lives of his family and colleagues a misery. His disorganization leads to an early heart attack and a confrontation with St Peter. By being given a second chance on Earth, he is able to learn the principles of time management in a way that viewers, many of whom will be unaware of their own faults, can easily relate to.

In **Part 2: Salvation** the manager has returned to Earth full of enthusiasm, but his inability to establish priorities and to delegate effectively lands him back in front of St Peter. The programme shows why managers should consider the actual purpose of their jobs, and not the function. They must learn how to schedule time for active tasks, while leaving time for reactive tasks. By delegating and retaining responsibility, they will make more effective use of their own time and that of their team, and contribute to everyone's motivation and morale.

Part 3: Divine Intervention picks up the story in the first two parts of the series but can be used as a stand-alone resource. It shows how effective managers can create time to focus on their teams.

Reflect and review

The now organized manager is called to St Peter, this time following an annual health check. Here he learns that his management style still leaves a lot to be desired, since he is failing to organize his team. Through highly memorable wrong-way, right-way scenarios, viewers will learn three steps to successful delegation.

It is the manager's role to ensure that each team member understands their purpose. The manager must define and identify their overall objective and their key result areas so that they know what is expected of them.

Individuals should be set standards to achieve, measurable either by quality, quantity or cost, so that both they and the manager know how they are doing.

And manager must agree targets with individual team members in order to help them develop and realise their potential, or to bring their performance back on track. Following the three steps, the manager will be able to improve the performance and results of individuals, the team and the organization.

Extension 3

Book	*Leadership Skills*
Author	John Adair
Edition	November 1998
Publisher	Chartered Institute of Personnel and Development (CIPD)

These extensions can be taken up via your ILM Centre. They will either have them or will arrange that you have access to them. However, it may be more convenient to check out the materials with your personnel or training people at work – they may well give you access. There are other good reasons for approaching your own people; for example, they will become aware of your interest and you can involve them in your development.

Reflect and review

4 Answers to self-assessment questions

Self-assessment 1 on page 18

1 Delegation means giving someone **RESPONSIBILITY** and **AUTHORITY** to act on your behalf.

2 If a task is delegated to you, you also need **RESOURCES** allocated to you in order to carry it out.

3 When you delegate a task, you have **OVERALL RESPONSIBILITY** for seeing that a job is done properly and on time.

4 Successful delegation helps to develop team members who are **COMPETENT**, **INVOLVED**, **COMMITTED** and **WELL-INFORMED**.

5 Delegation enables team leaders to draw on the expertise of team members and so improve **DECISION-MAKING**.

6 Time spent delegating is time well spent because:

- it involves developing the competence of team members; this is an important management responsibility;
- it enables you to pass on low to medium priority jobs to others and so concentrate your efforts on high priority work.

7 The term 'span of control' describes the number of people a supervisor is responsible for.

8 Here is the completed diagram:

Preparing to delegate
- Decide what to delegate
- Select team members

Carrying out the delegation
- Set objectives
- Plan
- Implement
- Monitor
- Review

Reflect and review

Self-assessment 2 on page 33

1 Reasons why managers may under-delegate are:

- they cannot be bothered to delegate, thinking it's easier to do it themselves;
- they think they do not have the time to delegate;
- they fear losing their reputation and are insecure in their job so don't want to share their power;
- they lack confidence and trust in their team members' abilities.

2 A sign that a manager is over-delegating is when he or she has NO CONTROL OVER THE TASKS THAT ARE DELEGATED.

3 The level of **CONTROL** you decide to take when you delegate is related to how much you **TRUST** the person to do a good job.

4 You can develop trust by going through the process of delegation, and helping the team member to be successful by using a high level of control at first.

Self-assessment 3 on page 58

1 I would argue that tasks c, d, e could definitely be delegated. You might also delegate task f.

2 Tasks a and b are definitely not suitable for delegation. Managers have responsibility for their team members' performance, and a manager's concern about lateness cannot be delegated to another member of the team. Organizations' staff grievance procedures usually specify the involvement of the manager in the first instance.

I would also argue that task g is not suitable for delegation, as your manager will expect you to do the job. However, you might want to involve team members in collecting and organizing the information.

Similarly, task h is not suitable, as you are discussing the needs of the whole of your team.

3 You might delegate a task to a team member who has not had experience in doing the task as a way of developing the team member's abilities.

4 You might delegate a task to a team member who has the expertise and experience in doing the task because the task needs to be done well, with few risks of mistakes. It may also be because you or other team members cannot offer much support for doing the job, or because you will not have time to take much direct control over the job.

Reflect and review

Self-assessment 4 on page 80

1 A SMART objective is:
   - specific;
   - measurable;
   - achievable;
   - relevant;
   - time bound.

2 When briefing a team member make sure that you and they **AGREE** all aspects of the task.

3 **MONITORING** involves collecting information about how well a task is going, and enables you or the team member to take action to prevent problems from becoming serious.

4 After the delegated task has been done, you should **REVIEW** its successes and failures, so that you can make improvements next time.

5 Part of a review involves giving **FEEDBACK** to the team member on his or her performance.

6 Here are the eight guidelines to follow.
   a Never give feedback when you are ANGRY. You need to be calm, thinking about solving any problem and moving forward.
   b Give PRAISE where it is due.
   c Encourage the person to whom you are giving feedback to CONTRIBUTE THEIR IDEAS.
   d Be specific about MISTAKES.
   e Criticize THE ACTION OR THE BEHAVIOUR, not the person.
   f Investigate the CAUSE of any difficulty.
   g Offer SUPPORT IN SOLVING THE PROBLEM.
   h End on a POSITIVE NOTE by looking forward to making improvements next time around.

Reflect and review

5 Answers to the quick quiz

Answer 1 Delegation means giving someone the **authority** and the **responsibility** to act on your behalf.

Answer 2 Delegation improves decision-making as it draws on the expertise of team members, who are actually carrying out the work of the section.

Answer 3 Team leaders keep overall responsibility for the work which they delegate by going through the process of delegation, and so retaining overall control of the job.

Answer 4 The process of effective delegation can be summarized as follows.

- Prepare for delegating by deciding:
  - what tasks can be delegated;
  - to whom.
- Carry out the delegation by:
  - setting and agreeing the objectives;
  - planning;
  - letting the team member carry out the task;
  - monitoring;
  - reviewing.

Answer 5 You can develop trust in your team by using high levels of control at first, in order to help the team member be successful, and then gradually using lower levels of control as your confidence and trust increase.

Answer 6 Over-delegation occurs when a supervisor gives too much responsibility for tasks to other people and loses control over the tasks

Answer 7 There are many possibilities here, depending on how you feel delegation will benefit you. For example, you may feel that a major benefit will be to give you more time to concentrate on your important work, help you to develop your staff or to develop your relationship with team members.

Answer 8 Delegation is a way of developing individuals in your team, improving their competence and skills. Besides this, delegation should help individuals feel well-informed, committed and involved.

Reflect and review

Answer 9 There will be tasks which you **have** to do yourself but, of the other tasks you do, you should delegate those that:

- your team members are competent to do;
- will help to develop team members;
- are of medium or low priority;
- are routine;
- are attractive to team members.

Answer 10 No. There are aspects of your work and responsibilities that you cannot delegate. Your own responsibility for health and safety is one of them. Your organization's policies and procedures may suggest others.

Answer 11 Someone who is delegated to do a task has to know what they will be working to achieve and by when. SMART objectives make this quite clear.

Answer 12 Resources include materials, equipment, money, people, time and information.

Answer 13 The briefing should seek to encourage a team member to feel committed and enthusiastic about the task. In the briefing you are seeking to reach agreement about the delegated task.

Answer 14 Monitoring allows you – and the person carrying out the task – to keep an eye on progress, to see where there might be potential problems, and to take corrective action, where appropriate, so that the task meets its objectives.

Answer 15 The purpose of giving feedback is to improve performance. This means that feedback should be given in such a way so as to encourage and motivate a team member.

6 Certificate

Completion of this certificate by an authorized person shows that you have worked through all the parts of this workbook and satisfactorily completed the assessments. The certificate provides a record of what you have done that may be used for exemptions or as evidence of prior learning against other nationally certificated qualifications.

Pergamon Flexible Learning and ILM are always keen to refine and improve their products. One of the key sources of information to help this process are people who have just used the product. If you have any information or views, good or bad, please pass these on.

INSTITUTE OF LEADERSHIP & MANAGEMENT
SUPERSERIES

Delegating Effectively

....

has satisfactorily completed this workbook

Name of signatory ....

Position ....

Signature ....

Date ....

Official stamp

Fourth Edition

INSTITUTE OF LEADERSHIP & MANAGEMENT
SUPERSERIES
FOURTH EDITION

Achieving Quality	0 7506 5874 6
Appraising Performance	0 7506 5838 X
Becoming More Effective	0 7506 5887 8
Budgeting for Better Performance	0 7506 5880 0
Caring for the Customer	0 7506 5840 1
Collecting Information	0 7506 5888 6
Commitment to Equality	0 7506 5893 2
Controlling Costs	0 7506 5842 8
Controlling Physical Resources	0 7506 5886 X
Delegating Effectively	0 7506 5816 9
Delivering Training	0 7506 5870 3
Effective Meetings at Work	0 7506 5882 7
Improving Efficiency	0 7506 5871 1
Information in Management	0 7506 5890 8
Leading Your Team	0 7506 5839 8
Making a Financial Case	0 7506 5892 4
Making Communication Work	0 7506 5875 4
Managing Change	0 7506 5879 7
Managing Lawfully – Health, Safety and Environment	0 7506 5841 X
Managing Lawfully – People and Employment	0 7506 5853 3
Managing Relationships at Work	0 7506 5891 6
Managing Time	0 7506 5877 0
Managing Tough Times	0 7506 5817 7
Marketing and Selling	0 7506 5837 1
Motivating People	0 7506 5836 3
Networking and Sharing Information	0 7506 5885 1
Organizational Culture and Context	0 7506 5884 3
Organizational Environment	0 7506 5889 4
Planning and Controlling Work	0 7506 5813 4
Planning Training and Development	0 7506 5860 6
Preventing Accidents	0 7506 5835 5
Project and Report Writing	0 7506 5876 2
Securing the Right People	0 7506 5822 3
Solving Problems	0 7506 5818 5
Storing and Retrieving Information	0 7506 5894 0
Understanding Change	0 7506 5878 9
Understanding Finance	0 7506 5815 0
Understanding Quality	0 7506 5881 9
Working In Teams	0 7506 5814 2
Writing Effectively	0 7506 5883 5

To order – phone us direct for prices and availability details
(please quote ISBNs when ordering) on 01865 888190